FATHERS
OF THE
BIBLE

Paul M. Miller

BARBOUR
PUBLISHING

Published by Barbour Publishing, Inc., P.O. Box 719, Uhrichsville, Ohio 44683, www.barbourbooks.com

Our mission is to publish and distribute inspirational products offering exceptional value and biblical encouragement to the masses.

Member of the
Evangelical Christian
Publishers Association

Contents

Introduction

Picture a home like all the rest in a subdivision— except for the twin boys who live inside. Their names are James and John, but the biblically alert neighbors call them "the sons of thunder". . .and for good reason.

Pushing open the back screen door the twins' father exits with one little boy in tow. The two seat themselves on the top step and watch the sun melt farther and farther under their neighbor's roof.

With a *bang*! the screen door is kicked open and the second "son of thunder" suddenly appears. Nimbly he scampers onto his father's lap. "Tell us a story, Pop," he says. John chimes in, laying his head on his father's shoulder, "Yeah, Dad, tell us one of your growing-up stories."

This scene could be replayed anywhere there are fathers and their kids spending time together. Maybe you've told your kids stories about your childhood—but maybe you've left out the best part. What do your kids know about your walk with God?

If you haven't answered that question, or haven't thought about it, or it's been awhile since you did, this book is for you. The scripture and devotionals that follow are all about Bible fathers who find themselves in sometimes amazing, sometimes tragic, always life-changing situations.

These are not bedtime stories for your kids but honest, inspirational, true stories meant just for you. These are focused devotionals and they have pointed lessons. Learn from these fathers. . .and then be determined to "walk the walk" for your kids' sake, as well as your own.

1. Once I Walked with God

Scripture from Genesis 1–4

And God said, Let us make man in our image, after our likeness. . . . And God saw every thing that he had made, and behold, it was very good. . . .

And the LORD God planted a garden eastward in Eden; and there he put the man whom he had formed . . . . And the LORD God commanded the man, saying, Of every tree of the garden thou mayest freely eat: But of the tree of the knowledge of good and evil, thou shalt not eat of it: for in the day that thou eatest thereof thou shalt surely die.

And the LORD God said, It is not good that the man should be alone; I will make him an help meet for him . . . . And the LORD God caused a deep sleep to fall upon Adam, and he slept: and he took one of his ribs, and closed up the flesh instead thereof; and the rib, which the LORD God had taken from man, made he a woman, and brought her unto the man. . . .

And they were both naked, the man and his wife, and were not ashamed. . . .

And [the serpent] said unto the woman, . . .hath God said, Ye shall not eat of every tree of the garden? And the woman said unto the serpent, We may eat of the fruit of the trees of the garden: but of the fruit of the tree which is in the midst of the garden, God hath said, Ye shall not eat of it, neither shall ye touch it, lest ye die.

And the serpent said unto the woman, Ye shall not surely die: For God doth know that in the day ye eat thereof, then your eyes shall be opened, and ye shall be as gods, knowing good and evil.

And when the woman saw that the tree was good for food, and that it was pleasant to the eyes, and a tree to be desired to make one wise, she took of the fruit thereof, and did eat, and gave also unto her husband with her; and he did eat.

And the eyes of them both were opened, and they knew that they were naked; and they sewed fig leaves together and made themselves aprons.

And they heard the voice of the LORD God walking in the garden in the cool of the day: and Adam and his wife hid. . . . And the LORD God called unto Adam, and said unto him, Where art thou?

And he said, I heard thy voice in the garden, and I was afraid, because I was naked; and I hid myself. And he said, Who told thee that thou wast naked? Hast thou eaten of the tree, whereof I commanded thee that thou shouldest not eat? And the man said, The woman whom thou gavest to be with me, she gave me of the tree, and I did eat. . . .

The woman said, The serpent beguiled me, and I did eat. . . .

Therefore the LORD God sent him forth from the garden of Eden, to till the ground from whence he was taken. . . .

And Adam knew Eve his wife; and she conceived, and bare Cain and. . .again bare his brother Abel.

Once I Walked with God
The Story of God and Adam

If Adam had made a timeline of his life, he might have used the initials B.E. ("Before Expulsion") and A.E. ("After Expulsion"). He would be referring, of course, to his once-blissful life in the Garden of Eden before he and his wife Eve were banished because of their sin against God.

Lying in a shelter east of Eden, their sons asleep, Adam and Eve probably reminisced about their garden home, gone forever. So many memories of contentment . . .the animals of every stripe, bowers of beauty, trees covered with every delectable fruit imaginable, and the closeness of their Creator, God. How many times did the couple shed tears over their decision to eat the fruit from that forbidden tree in the center of the garden?

The story of Adam reveals that it is possible to destroy a relationship—both human and divine—by allowing self-centeredness to raise its serpentine head.

When God was finished forming the first man, He gave him the name Adam and moved him into the Garden of Eden. For a while, Adam lived peaceably amid his natural surroundings until God decided that he should not be alone. God then created a wife for Adam whom Adam named Eve.

In the Garden of Eden, the man and woman were allowed to do what they wished. Adam and Eve could pick the flowers, nibble the grapes, feed kumquats to the monkeys, and bathe in pomegranate juice! Each day was a delight and an adventure.

There was, however, one restriction established by God, one that didn't seem so limiting at the time. But that would change.

We don't know this, but likely Adam's greatest joy was at evening when God called for him and they'd stroll through the garden. Perhaps they'd talk about how Adam was doing with the garden or in naming the animals. It is certainly possible that one evening God asked Adam if Eve understood about the tree of the knowledge of good and evil. Like any good husband, Adam probably assured God that he had it all under control, that Eve understood that the consequences of doing so meant death.

Keep in mind that Adam and Eve were not perfect: Like us, they had the ability to make choices, from deciding what they'd have for supper to eating from a forbidden tree.

Eve's decision to do just that was the beginning of the end. By eating the fruit of the tree of the knowledge of good and evil, Eve fulfilled her own appetite and then discovered the need to include Adam in her decision.

Imagine Adam and Eve remembering that momentous day when they disobeyed God. What shame they must have felt when they let themselves be deceived by the serpent (Satan in disguise)!

Like men and women today, they believed that they could better themselves by disobeying God. What they were left with was the bitter knowledge that they had separated themselves from their Father.

Once I Walked with God

Think It Over

If you are a father with a forgiven, or perhaps an unforgiven, past, what should you tell your children about your wayward days? How might that information help or hinder them?

Is there a way in which you, as a father, can be "the voice of God" to your kids? Or can you?

How would Adam's response to Eve and the forbidden fruit work today?

If Cain and Abel had been in the Garden of Eden with their parents, do you think the story would have taken a different turn? How do kids affect parents' decision-making powers?

And God saw every thing that he had made,
and, behold, it was very good.
GENESIS 1:31

2. Am I My Brother's Keeper?

Scripture from Genesis 4

And Adam knew Eve his wife; and she conceived, and bare Cain, and said, I have gotten a man from the LORD. And she again bare his brother Abel. And Abel was a keeper of sheep, but Cain was a tiller of the ground.

And in process of time it came to pass, that Cain brought of the fruit of the ground an offering unto the LORD. And Abel, he also brought of the firstlings of his flock and of the fat thereof. And the LORD had respect unto Abel and to his offering: but unto Cain and to his offering he had not respect. And Cain was very wroth, and his countenance fell.

And the LORD said unto Cain, Why art thou wroth? and why is thy countenance fallen?

If thou doest well, shalt thou not be accepted? and if thou doest not well, sin lieth at the door. And unto thee shall be his desire, and thou shalt rule over him.

And Cain talked with Abel his brother: and it came to pass, when they were in the field, that Cain rose up against Abel his brother, and slew him.

And the LORD said unto Cain, Where is Abel thy brother? And he said, I know not: Am I my brother's keeper?

And he said, What hast thou done? The voice of thy brother's blood crieth unto me from the ground. And now art thou cursed from the earth, which hath opened her mouth to receive thy brother's blood from thy hand; When thou tillest the ground, it shall not henceforth yield unto thee her strength; a fugitive and a vagabond shalt thou be in the earth.

And Cain said unto the LORD, My punishment is greater than I can bear. Behold, thou hast driven me out this day from the face of the earth; and from thy face shall I be hid; and I shall be a fugitive and a vagabond in the earth; and it shall come to pass, that every one that findeth me shall slay me.

And the LORD said unto him, Therefore whosoever slayeth Cain, vengeance shall be taken on him sevenfold. And the LORD set a mark upon Cain, lest any finding him should kill him.

And Cain went out from the presence of the LORD, and dwelt in the land of Nod, on the east of Eden.

Am I My Brother's Keeper?
The Story of Adam and His Sons

It's not easy to rate Adam as a father. We do know this: Adam and Eve's first two sons were relatively close in age to one another and were born and grew to manhood outside of the Garden of Eden. With their father they labored hard and long, Cain working as a farmer, and Abel as a shepherd.

Acquainted as we are with the story of Eden—its forbidden fruit, the newly minted couple, Satan's ego-feeding temptation, and Adam and Eve's eventual banishment—there is no information provided about any interaction between Adam and his boys.

Yet, as with most Old Testament sagas, the story of Adam and his sons has undeniable truths for today. Too often we stumble over historicity and lose the larger picture—the facts that God wants dads like us to understand.

Fact one: "My son, hear the instruction of thy father" (Proverbs 1:8).

Fact two: "The heavens are the LORD's: but the earth hath he given to the children of men" (Psalm 115:16).

God has entrusted the earth to you and to your children. So what does He expect of you? To live responsibly for your family and to pass down your Christian faith to your children. When a father fails to do this, or when a child fails to grasp biblical truths, the effects may be felt for generations to come.

That said, it seems inconceivable that murder could enter the lives of the first family created by God, and that a man one generation removed from the blissful setting of Eden could take the life of his brother.

Remember, though, that Cain and Abel weren't born until after Adam and Eve were banished from Eden. They had no memory of their father walking with God. Cain was the older son, and perhaps the more aggressive. In Hebrew his name means "acquisition," while Abel's name means "temporary." Yet all this doesn't explain why one son would commit murder, especially living under Adam's roof.

Readers of Genesis can assume that Adam taught Cain and Abel about their responsibilities to God. Even when they were eking out a living, which was nearly always, we can assume that Adam made sure to make offerings to God.

A casual reading of the text makes one question why God accepted Abel's animal offering while Cain's fruit offering was rejected. We learn that Abel's offering was pleasing to God because he offered it with faith (Hebrews 11:4), while Cain's offering appears to have been one given grudgingly and thoughtlessly. Without possessing faith, he thought he could get away with it. When God rejected Cain's offering, Cain was filled with jealousy and murdered his brother.

When God questioned him about Abel, Cain's answer was, "Am I my brother's keeper?" In other words, "I will not take responsibility for my brother's death." God ordered Cain into exile, and so he went into the land of Nod, east of Eden.

The lesson? Fathers who have kids who obey, more often than not, are kids who see God obeyed in their families. God wants us to be responsible dads, and that means trusting our lives and our futures to Him—and then imparting those truths to our children.

Am I My Brother's Keeper?

Think It Over

Cain's flippant answer to God is a contemporary attitude that is no respecter of age. In this day of casual relationships, how does a father teach his kids to honor God? How do you demonstrate your respect for God?

Many who write about this scripture agree that a one-word theme for the passage is *responsibility*. What is the motivation for your sense of responsibility? How do you model it at home?

We don't know what kind of dad Adam was, but we do know that Abel possessed faith and that faith pleased God. Abel undoubtedly was the beneficiary of Adam's close relationship with God.

How are you contributing to the success you hope for your child?

> *A sound heart is the life of the flesh:*
> *but envy the rottenness of the bones.*
> PROVERBS 14:30

3. A Father's Odyssey
Scripture from Genesis 4 and 5

And Cain went out from the presence of the LORD, and dwelt in the land of Nod, on the east of Eden.

And Cain knew his wife; and she conceived, and bare Enoch. . . .

And Enoch lived sixty and five years, and begat Methuselah: and Enoch walked with God after he begat Methuselah three hundred years, and begat sons and daughters.

And all the days of Enoch were three hundred sixty and five years: and Enoch walked with God; and he was not; for God took him.

And Methuselah lived an hundred eighty and seven years, and begat Lamech. And Methuselah lived after he begat Lamech seven hundred eighty and two years, and begat sons and daughters.

And all the days of Methuselah were nine hundred sixty and nine years: and he died.

And Lamech lived an hundred eighty and two years, and begat a son: and he called his name Noah, saying, This same shall comfort us concerning our work and toil of our hands, because of the ground which the LORD hath cursed [because of Adam and Eve's disobedience].

And Lamech lived after he begat Noah five hundred ninety and five years, and begat sons and daughters.

And all the days of Lamech were seven hundred seventy and seven years: and he died.

A Father's Odyssey
The Story of Lamech and Noah

Lamech was part of the ninth generation after Adam through Seth, Adam's third son. Because Seth was born after Abel's murder, his parents bestowed on him a name that means "replacement." Very quickly many sons and daughters were born and the earth became populated.

When Seth was 105 years old, he had a son, whom he named Enos. Adam's genealogy continues on to a familiar name, Methuselah, who, when he died at age 969, became the oldest man in history. Of greater import is that Methuselah had the distinction of being Lamech's father and grandfather to Noah (of Noah and the ark fame).

As time passed, Lamech discovered that their familiar community was changing. It became unpopular for a man to worship the one true God and to put into practice values that had a wholesome effect on his family.

Before Lamech realized this, God, of course, was aware of these changes. As the earth's population increased, more and more young men and women were choosing to live in sin. Immorality was sweeping over His creation like a flood.

With sorrow, God warned His creation, "My Spirit will not contend with man forever" (Genesis 6:3 NIV). Then, like any heartbroken parent whose words are ignored, He was forced to make good His threat. "I will wipe mankind, whom I have created, from the face of the earth" (Genesis 6:7 NIV).

That is, all humankind except Lamech's son Noah and his family: Only Noah had found favor in the eyes of the Lord.

Genesis doesn't tell us when Noah announced to his family that God told him to build an ark to save his family and pairs of all the creatures on earth. But is it too far-fetched to believe that son Noah might have gone to his father, Lamech, and told him what God's plan was, before announcing it to the rest of the family? Lamech would not live to see the flood, but he did live to see his son grow to become a true man of God.

Fathers who have living Christian fathers are fortunate. Those elderly dads have a wealth of support available to their sons. A pastor recently read a letter to his dad on Father's Day. Here is an excerpt: "As a boy I know you prayed for me—I could hear your booming voice. Now as a man, Dad, I still count on your prayer support."

What father among us wouldn't be overjoyed to know that his son, like Noah, "found favor in the eyes of the LORD" (Genesis 6:8 NIV)?

A Father's Odyssey

Think It Over

The gaps between generations can be troublesome chasms. How does the story of Lamech and Noah relate to you and your family relationships? Do you have any Lamechs in your home? Are you a Lamech?

For those fathers who do not have a Christian "genealogy" to look back on, where can you find support and strength in times of crisis? Read Proverbs 24:3–4. Think about the words "wisdom" and "building" and then ask yourself, what is the house?

What helps a father to accept that his son is doing something (becoming someone) even greater than he? Lamech knew that during those years Noah was at home, he was being prepared. Can you relate to this?

It's easy to forget that before these great characters in the Old Testament made headlines, they were the product of homes. What qualities are being molded in your children as a result of living under your roof?

But continue thou in the things which thou hast learned and hast been assured of, knowing of whom thou hast learned them.
2 TIMOTHY 3:14

4. The Promise and a Rainbow

Scripture from Genesis 6–9

But Noah found grace in the eyes of the LORD. . . . Noah was a just man and perfect in his generations, and Noah walked with God.

And Noah begat three sons, Shem, Ham, and Japheth.

The earth also was corrupt before God, and the earth was filled with violence. And God looked upon the earth, and, behold, it was corrupt; for all flesh had corrupted his way upon the earth. And God said unto Noah, The end of all flesh is come before me; for the earth is filled with violence through them; and behold, I will destroy them with the earth.

Make thee an ark of gopher wood. . . . The length of the ark shall be three hundred cubits [450 feet], the breadth of it fifty cubits [75 feet], and the height of it thirty cubits [45 feet]. . . .

And, behold, I, even I, do bring a flood of waters upon the earth, to destroy all flesh, wherein is the breath of life, from under heaven; and every thing that is in the earth shall die.

But with thee will I establish my covenant; and thou shalt come into the ark, thou, and thy sons, and thy wife, and thy sons' wives with thee. And of every living thing of all flesh, two of every sort shalt thou bring into the ark, to keep them alive with thee; they shall be male and female. . . .

Thus did Noah; according to all that God commanded him, so did he. . . .

And Noah was six hundred years old when the flood

of waters was upon the earth. And Noah went in, and his sons, and his wife, and his sons' wives with him, into the ark, because of the waters of the flood. . . .

And the flood was forty days upon the earth; and the waters increased, and bare up the ark, and it was lift up above the earth. . . .

And all flesh died that moved upon the earth, both of fowl, and of cattle, and of beast, and of every creeping thing that creepeth upon the earth, and every man. . . . Noah only remained alive, and they that were with him in the ark. And the waters prevailed upon the earth an hundred and fifty days.

God remembered Noah, and every living thing, and all the cattle that was with him in the ark: and God made a wind to pass over the earth, and the waters assuaged. . . . And the ark rested. . .upon the mountains of Ararat. . . .

And God spake unto Noah, saying, Go forth of the ark, thou, and thy wife, and thy sons, and thy sons' wives with thee. . .and Noah went forth. . . . Every beast, every creeping thing, and every fowl, and whatsoever creepeth upon the earth, after their kinds, went forth out of the ark.

And Noah builded up an altar unto the LORD; and took of every clean beast, and of every clean fowl, and offered burnt offerings on the altar. And the LORD smelled a sweet savour; and the LORD said in his heart, I will not again curse the ground any more for man's sake. . . .

And I [God], behold, I establish my covenant with you, and with your seed after you. . . . I do set my bow [rainbow] in the cloud, and it shall be for a token of a covenant between me and the earth. . .and the waters shall no more become a flood to destroy all flesh.

The Promise and a Rainbow
The Story of Noah and His Sons

Umpteen generations before Noah was born, God created the world and Adam—the father of humankind. And He said it was all "good."

But now, many generations later, God is about to wipe His creation off the face of the earth and start all over again, with Noah as a sort of second father of humankind.

You can imagine the tensions around the Noah home when he announced to the family that the Lord had told him to build an ark of monumental dimensions—because a flood was coming!

Sons being sons, no doubt they had all kinds of objections. Perhaps their practical wives drew attention to the fact that in a desert region it didn't rain very much. And what about Noah's plan to save the animals? They could only roll their eyes at that.

Still, for a man like Noah who had found grace in the eyes of the Lord, how could he throw cold water on God's directive? Can't you imagine old Lamech holding up a shaky hand and declaring, "Listen to your father! He has found favor with God."

When the first raindrops began to fall and the neighbors looked to heaven wondering what was happening. . . when the raindrops didn't stop for forty days and forty nights. . .when the world's population was wiped off the face of the earth (except for the Noah family secure in their floating home and zoo). . .when at last Noah popped open a window and released a bird. . .and when that bird flew back dry with greenery in his beak. . .Noah was able to declare, "It's over!"

To all those who have ever dreamed of climbing Mount Ararat to find the remains of Noah's ark, understand that of greater consequence than an ancient piece of gopher wood is a sign in the sky, often observed after a cleansing rain. It's the rainbow God placed there as a reminder of His love for us—and a pledge that never again would He send a flood to destroy the world.

After such an epic experience, what happened to the sons of Noah? The youngest and oldest, Japheth and Shem, remained in Noah's good graces, while second son Ham ridiculed his father to his brothers and was cursed.

After the flood, Noah lived 350 more years, which made his entire life span a whopping 950 years.

Sadly, humankind did not return to God. Like those in Noah's day, we continue to worship false gods and flaunt sinful behavior. Whatever we could learn from Noah's story has been diluted and relegated mostly to children's storybooks. Yet, the words of Jesus, God's Son, remind us that the next worldwide judgment is near: "And as it was in the days of Noe [Noah], so shall it be also in the days of the Son of man" (Luke 17:26).

The Promise and a Rainbow

In a fictional short story based on Noah and the ark, neighbors help him build the ark. As the story goes, when the flood waters deepened, the helpful neighbors pounded on the ark door and pleaded, "Let us in, we helped you build this boat." Noah replied, "But you didn't believe." What does this have to say about your salvation?

No doubt, in the eyes of the community, Noah looked foolish building the ark and talking of a flood to come that would wipe them out. Probably when the rains started, there were those still laughing, thinking that Noah was nothing but an old fool. How are you being a "fool" for Jesus Christ? Whose "fool" are you? Does the fear of foolishness keep you from sharing Christ with your neighbors?

Genesis 8:1 reads, "And God remembered Noah." What comforting words those are, to know that in the midst of all of the chaos of the world, God remembers the individual who trusts in Him! Read Matthew 10:29–31.

Summarize what this story of Noah teaches. How does it relate directly to you as a father. . .as a son. . .as a husband . . .as an in-law?

And as it was in the days of Noe, so shall it be also in the days of the Son of man.
LUKE 17:26

5. One for Three—Not Bad!

Scripture from Genesis 11–12

These are the generations of Shem [Noah's son]: Shem was an hundred years old, and begat Arphaxad two years after the flood. And Shem lived after he begat Arphaxad five hundred years, and begat sons and daughters.

And Arphaxad. . .begat Salah. . . . And Salah. . . begat Eber. . . . Eber. . .begat Peleg. . . . Peleg. . .begat Reu. . . . Reu. . .begat Serug. . . . Serug. . .begat Nahor. . . and Nahor. . .begat Terah. . . .

And Terah lived seventy years, and begat Abram, Nahor, and Haran.

Now these are the generations of Terah: Terah begat Abram, Nahor, and Haran; and Haran begat Lot. And Haran died before his father Terah in the land of his nativity, in Ur of the Chaldees.

And Abram and Nahor took them wives: the name of Abram's wife was Sarai; and the name of Nahor's wife, Milcah, the daughter of Haran, the father of Milcah, and the father of Iscah.

But Sarai was barren; she had no child.

And Terah took Abram his son, and Lot the son of Haran his son's son, and Sarai his daughter in law, his son Abram's wife; and they went forth with them from Ur of the Chaldees, to go into the land of Canaan; and they came unto Haran, and dwelt there.

The days of Terah were two hundred and five years: and Terah died in Haran.

Now the LORD had said unto Abram, Get thee out of thy country, and from thy kindred, and from thy father's house, unto a land that I will shew thee: And I will make of thee a great nation, and I will bless thee, and make thy name great; and thou shalt be a blessing: And I will bless them that bless thee, and curse him that curseth thee: and in thee shall all families of the earth be blessed.

> *The greatest gift I ever had came from God—*
> *And I call him Dad!*
> ANONYMOUS

One for Three—Not Bad!
The Story of Terah and Abram

To read through the family tree of an Old Testament patriarch and his forebears requires the intrepid fortitude of an Indiana Jones. It's no small task to climb through the tangled branches and offshoots to reach a recognizable relative.

Take Terah, for instance. His tree is impressive, though not overgrown with celebrity names. But who needs those when the patriarch Abram is your son and Lot, your grandson?

Still, there are two other names in Terah's tree that are intriguing: Nahor and Haran, Terah's other sons and brothers to Abram. Reference books and the Bible itself are rather quiet about them. We do know that Nahor married a woman by the name of Milcah, and they settled in the area of Haran. That's about it.

Haran doesn't fare much better in lines of copy. His distinction is that he died in Ur and that he had three children: Milcah (probably named for her aunt), Iscah, and Lot. Lot! Yes, the Lot, whose wife turned into a pillar of salt. Like Terah, one biggie out of three wasn't bad for Haran.

So, what is there to learn from the people in this family tree? What can a contemporary father take away from these names and the lives behind them?

If there had been an ancient version of Father's Day, what kind of messages would Nahor and Haran have scribbled in their cards to Dad? "Sorry I'm not getting the grades Abram's getting," or, "One of these days I'm going to make you really proud of me!"

Most wise dads who live close to their children are aware of the jealousies and competition taking place within the family. Terah probably knew that it wasn't easy for two of his sons to live in the other's shadow.

So touching are the words describing Haran's early death: "And Haran died before his father Terah in the land of his nativity, in Ur of the Chaldees" (Genesis 11:28). It's the father who should precede the son in death, not the other way around. True, Terah was quite old when Haran died and left his wife and three children in Ur, but even an old man could ask the question, "Why him, Lord? So young, and such a fine husband and father. Why not me? I'm all used up. My days are behind me. You could have taken me."

Terah had a right to be proud of his boys, no matter what their achievements or how they were used by God. Each made his own contribution to the family. And each had his name inscribed in God's Book.

One for Three—Not Bad!

Think It Over

In today's economy, three kids is quite a household—that's three growing appetites, just for starters. Read Philippians 4:19. How can you relate that verse to your family?

A father who is able to make each one of his kids feel like the family favorite is blessed. What is the secret behind making each son or daughter feel equal in your sight?

How can the father who has lost a child keep the memory of that son or daughter alive? What does he owe his other children?

When one has a truly gifted child, how can that gift be encouraged, but not to the neglect of the other children?

The LORD shall increase you more and more, you and your children. Ye are blessed of the LORD which made heaven and earth. The heaven, even the heavens, are the LORD's; but the earth hath he given to the children of men.
PSALM 115:14–16

6. Ishmael's Father

Scripture from Genesis 16, 21

Now Sarai Abram's wife bare him no children: and she had an handmaid, an Egyptian, whose name was Hagar. And Sarai said unto Abram, Behold now, the LORD hath restrained me from bearing: I pray thee, go in unto my maid; it may be that I may obtain children by her. And Abram hearkened to the voice of Sarai.

And Sarai Abram's wife took Hagar her maid the Egyptian, after Abram had dwelt ten years in the land of Canaan, and gave her to her husband Abram to be his wife. And he went in unto Hagar, and she conceived: and when she saw that she had conceived, her mistress was despised in her eyes.

And Sarai said unto Abram, My wrong be upon thee: I have given my maid into thy bosom; and when she saw that she had conceived, I was despised in her eyes: the LORD judge between me and thee.

But Abram said unto Sarai, Behold, thy maid is in thine hand; do to her as it pleaseth thee. And when Sarai dealt hardly with her, she fled from her face.

And the angel of the LORD found [Hagar] by a fountain of water in the wilderness, by the fountain in the way to Shur. And he said, Hagar, Sarai's maid, whence camest thou? and whither wilt thou go? And she said, I flee from the face of my mistress Sarai.

And the angel of the LORD said unto her, Return to thy mistress, and submit thyself under her hands. And the angel of the LORD said unto her, I will multiply thy seed exceedingly, that it shall not be numbered for multitude...

Behold, thou art with child and shalt bare a son, and shalt call his name Ishmael; because the LORD hath heard thy affliction. And he will be a wild man; his hand will be against every man, and every man's hand against him; and he shall dwell in the presence of all his brethren.

And [Hagar] called the name of the LORD that spake to her, Thou God seest me, for she said, Have I also here looked after him that seeth me? . . .

And Hagar bare Abram a son: and Abram called his son's name, which Hagar bare, Ishmael. And Abram was fourscore and six years old when Hagar bare Ishmael.

[Abraham and Sarah—God changed their names from Abram and Sarai—were later blessed with the birth of their own son, Isaac. Meanwhile, Ishmael grew and was weaned.]

And Sarah saw the son of Hagar the Egyptian, which she had born unto Abraham, mocking. Wherefore she said unto Abraham, Cast out this bondwoman and her son: for the son of this bondwoman shall not be heir with my son, even with Isaac.

And the thing was very grievous in Abraham's sight because of his son. And God said unto Abraham, Let it not be grievous in thy sight because of the lad, and because of thy bondwoman; in all that Sarah hath said unto thee, hearken unto her voice; for in Isaac shall thy seed be called. And also of the son of the bondwoman will I make a nation, because he is thy seed.

And Abraham rose up early in the morning, and took bread, and a bottle of water, and gave it unto Hagar, putting it on her shoulder, and the child, and sent her away.

Ishmael's Father
The Story of Abraham and Ishmael

There used to be a song that kids sang at church camp that went something like this:

> *Father Abraham had many sons,*
> *Many sons had Father Abraham.*
> *I am one of them,*
> *And so are you,*
> *So let's just praise the Lord.*

When we sang "many," we had no idea how many that was! Little did we know that Abraham means "father of a multitude." That's how many!

The story of Abraham, the father of the Jewish people, begins with God's command, "Get thee out of thy country [Ur of the Chaldees], and from thy kindred, and from thy father's house [Terah], unto a land that I will shew thee" (Genesis 12:1).

Abram, as he was then known, would have to leave behind everything except his wife Sarai, as she was then called, his nephew Lot, and all the possessions they had accumulated. So, at seventy-five years old, Abram set out from Haran as an immigrant.

En route to the land to which God was leading them, a famine broke out, endangering Abram's and Lot's cattle, so they detoured to Egypt. From there they moved on to the plain of Jordan and there Lot stayed, while Abram and Sarai settled in Canaan.

Always in the back of their minds was the fact that Abram and Sarai were childless. To ease her pain, and as a quick solution to an embarrassing problem, Sarai offered her servant Hagar to Abraham to bear his child. After Hagar became pregnant, though, a hatred arose between the servant and her mistress, resulting in Sarai's mistreatment of Hagar and the servant's eventual escape.

While running away from Sarai, Hagar was intercepted by an angel of the Lord, who asked, "Hagar, servant of Sarai, where have you come from, and where are you going?"

Hagar's truthful answer was, "I'm running away from my mistress Sarai."

The angel told her to return to Sarai and to put up with her mistreatment because God had a plan for Ishmael, her soon-to-be-born son. The angel went on to tell her that her son would be a wild man, one who would struggle to get along with others. (In other words, no teacher of his would ever report, "Ishmael works well with other children"!)

Years later, after the birth of her son Isaac, Sarah finally got rid of Hagar and Ishmael after she saw the older boy, in the words of scripture, "mocking" Isaac. As a result, she demanded that Abraham send them away.

This matter distressed Abraham greatly, but God spoke to him in his unhappiness. "Do not be so distressed about the boy and your maidservant. . . . It is through Isaac that your offspring will be reckoned."

To ease Abraham's concern for his son Ishmael, God assured him, "I will make [him] into a nation also, because he is your offspring."

In prompt obedience to God, the very next morning, Abraham bade Hagar and Ishmael goodbye. Abraham had obeyed God when He said to leave his home and he obeyed Him now. (See Genesis 16:7–12 and 21:11–13 NIV.)

Ishmael's Father

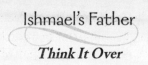

Think It Over

A jealous wife can make life miserable for her husband. Do you think Sarah ever acknowledged that it was her idea for Abraham to father a child by her servant? Read Proverbs 14:30. Do you have "a sound heart"?

Evidently Sarah saw Ishmael as a threat to Isaac. In that day, driving the mother and son away was, in fact, disinheriting them. As a father, what responsibilities do you have to a second family? Is there more expected than a monthly check and regular visits? What spiritual responsibility does a dad have to children of a former marriage?

Bible commentators often call attention to Abraham's promptness in carrying out the Lord's instruction (see Genesis 21:12–14). In this way, Abraham is modeling behavior that God expects.

Does the story of Abraham and Ishmael have anything to say to fathers who have children from a previous marriage? What do you feel are Abraham's strengths in dealing with Ishmael?

Hear, ye children, the instruction of a father,
and attend to know understanding.
For I give you good doctrine, forsake ye not my law.
PROVERBS 4:1–2

7. God Will Provide

Scripture from Genesis 21–22

And the LORD visited Sarah as he had said, and the LORD did unto Sarah as he had spoken. For Sarah conceived, and bare Abraham a son in his old age, at the set time of which God had spoken to him. And Abraham called the name of his son that was born unto him, whom Sarah bare to him, Isaac. . . .

And it came to pass after these things, that God did tempt Abraham, and said unto him, Abraham: and he said, Behold, here I am.

And he said, Take now thy son, thine only son Isaac, whom thou lovest, and get thee into the land of Moriah; and offer him there for a burnt offering upon one of the mountains which I will tell thee of.

And Abraham rose up early in the morning, and saddled his ass, and took two of his young men with him, and Isaac his son, and clave the wood for the burnt offering, and rose up, and went unto the place of which God had told him.

Then on the third day Abraham lifted up his eyes, and saw the place afar off.

And Abraham said unto his young men, Abide ye here with the ass; and I and the lad will go yonder and worship, and come again to you.

And Abraham took the wood of the burnt offering, and laid it upon Isaac his son; and he took the fire in his hand, and a knife; and they went both of them together.

And Isaac spake unto Abraham his father, and said, My father: and he said, Here am I, my son. And he said,

Behold the fire and the wood: but where is the lamb for a burnt offering?

And Abraham said, My son, God will provide himself a lamb for a burnt offering: so they went both of them together.

And they came to the place which God had told him of; and Abraham built an altar there, and laid the wood in order, and bound Isaac his son, and laid him on the altar upon the wood.

And Abraham stretched forth his hand, and took the knife to slay his son.

And the angel of the LORD called unto him out of heaven, and said, Abraham, Abraham: and he said, Here am I.

And [the angel] said, Lay not thine hand upon the lad, neither do thou any thing unto him: for now I know that thou fearest God, seeing thou hast not withheld thy son, thine only son from me.

And Abraham lifted up his eyes, and looked, and behold behind him a ram caught in a thicket by his horns: and Abraham went and took the ram, and offered him up for a burnt offering in the stead of his son.

My father died many years ago,
and yet when something special happens to me,
I talk to him secretly not really knowing whether he hears,
but it makes me feel better to half believe it.
NATASHA JOSEFOWITZ

God Will Provide
The Story of Abraham and Isaac

"Isaac, my son, you and I are going to take a trip together. God has told me to take you to Mount Moriah to make a sacrifice."

That's the paraphrased beginning of one of the most wrenching moments between father and son in history.

Isaac was God's gift to Abraham and Sarah long after Sarah's childbearing years were over. He was the fulfillment of a promise God had made to them. Years after Isaac's birth, though, God tested Abraham's faith by asking him to sacrifice his own son.

While artists have depicted Isaac at this time as a wondering little boy or a bright-eyed adolescent, his age is not revealed in Genesis. Most Bible scholars place Isaac in his late teens or early twenties.

Likely, Isaac knew this was not some kind of father-son camping trip. To worship such a distance away was unusual. Little did he or his father know that this was to be a foreshadowing of the ultimate story of salvation: a mountain (Calvary), a Son (Jesus), His Father (God), and a sacrifice (Jesus' crucifixion).

The conversation on the way to Moriah was filled with tension. At some point Isaac asks (and I'm paraphrasing here), "The burnt offering, Dad? I know we have the wood—I'm carrying it on my back! But where's the lamb to sacrifice?"

Of course Abraham is aware that the Lord expects him to sacrifice Isaac, but the boy is puzzled—and probably growing more concerned by the moment. "That's all right, son. God Himself will provide the lamb."

As Mount Moriah looms in front of them, with Isaac bearing wood on his back, father and son trudge up the trail to the place of sacrifice.

"We need to erect an altar, Isaac. Gather some stones and I'll help you build us one."

With Isaac occupied, Abraham may have begun a one-sided discussion with God. By the time the altar is prepared, Abraham is settled in his heart that he must obey. The Bible account of this historical event is silent on whatever father-son dialogue took place before the old man bound the boy and laid him on the altar.

Abraham reaches for his knife, raises it in the air. . . and then an angel speaks!

"Stop, Abraham! Do not lay a hand on the boy. Now I know that you fear God, because you were willing to obey; you did not withhold Isaac from God."

And what did God provide instead of Isaac? A ram that was caught in a thicket—and more. One day, hundreds of years later, God would watch His own Son climb a hill with a wooden cross on his back, the Lamb of God who takes away the sins of the world.

God Will Provide

Think It Over

In your role as a father, how have you been tested? There is an old gospel song that says, "Trust and obey, for there's no other way to be happy in Jesus, but to trust and obey." Relate that to you and your family.

In today's world, a father would be institutionalized at the very least if he claimed God had told him to sacrifice his child. What does it take for God to get your attention? What kind of demands does He put on you? How does He speak to you?

The foundation of Abraham and Isaac's story is the promise "God will provide." How can this promise be part of your personal life and your family's?

Read Ephesians 5:8. To those who "trust and obey," God promises that we will live "as children of light." How can God's Spirit generate more light in your family?

Behold, to obey is better than sacrifice,
and to hearken than the fat of rams.
1 SAMUEL 15:22

8. A Son's Hairy Tale
Scripture from Genesis 27

And it came to pass, that when Isaac was old, and his eyes were dim, so that he could not see, he called Esau his eldest son, and said unto him, My son: and he said unto him, Behold, here am I.

And [Isaac] said, Behold now, I am old, I know not the day of my death: Now therefore take, I pray thee, thy weapons, thy quiver and thy bow, and go out to the field, and take me some venison; and make me savoury meat, such as I love, and bring it to me, that I may eat; that my soul may bless thee before I die.

And Rebekah heard when Isaac spake to Esau his son. And Esau went to the field to hunt for venison, and to bring it. And Rebekah spake unto Jacob her son, saying, Behold, I heard thy father speak unto Esau thy brother, saying, Bring me venison, and make me savoury meat, that I may eat, and bless thee before the LORD before my death.

Now therefore, my son, obey my voice according to that which I command thee. Go now to the flock, and fetch me from thence two good kids of the goats; and I will make them savoury meat for thy father, such as he loveth; and thou shalt bring it to thy father, that he may eat, and that he may bless thee before his death.

And Jacob said to Rebekah his mother, Behold, Esau my brother is a hairy man, and I am a smooth man: My father peradventure will feel me, and I shall seem to him as a deceiver; and I shall bring a curse upon me, and not a blessing.

And his mother said unto him, Upon me be thy

curse, my son; only obey my voice, and go fetch me them. And he went, and fetched, and brought them to his mother; and his mother made savoury meat, such as his father loved. And Rebekah took goodly raiment of her eldest son Esau, which were with her in the house, and put them upon Jacob her younger son: and she put the skins of the kids of the goats upon his hands, and upon the smooth of his neck: and she gave the savoury meat and the bread, which she had prepared, into the hand of her son Jacob.

And he came unto his father, and said, My father: and he said, Here am I; who art thou, my son?

And Jacob said unto his father, I am Esau thy first born; I have done according as thou badest me: arise, I pray thee, sit and eat of my venison, that thy soul may bless me.

And Isaac said unto his son, How is it that thou hast found it so quickly, my son? And he said, Because the Lord thy God brought it to me.

And Isaac said unto Jacob, Come near, I pray thee, that I may feel thee, my son, whether thou be my very son Esau or not.

And Jacob went near unto Isaac his father; and he felt him, and said, The voice is Jacob's voice, but the hands are the hands of Esau. And he discerned him not, because his hands were hairy, as his brother Esau's hands: so he blessed him. And he said, Art thou my very son Esau? And he said, I am. . . .

As soon as Isaac had made an end of blessing Jacob, and Jacob was yet scarce gone out from the presence of Isaac his father, that Esau his brother came in from his hunting. . . . And Esau hated Jacob.

A Son's Hairy Tale
The Story of Isaac and Jacob and Esau

The story of Isaac and Jacob and Esau sounds like some of those dramas from the early days of radio, the ones that were known as "cliff-hangers." At the close of this fifteen-minute episode, an announcer comes on and says the following in an urgent voice:

ANNOUNCER:
As Jacob stands there before his blind old dad pretending to be his hairy brother Jacob, he can hear his brother's footsteps coming closer to the house. In just a minute, Esau will burst in and you'll hear him say. . .

ESAU:
Hey, what's going on here? Why do you have that hairy goatskin on your arms, Jacob? What are you trying to do?

ANNOUNCER:
Tune in tomorrow night—same time, same station—for the answers to Esau's frantic questions.

Isaac is now an old man whose eyes aren't what they used to be. He's been married to Rebekah for a lot of years. They have twin sons, Jacob and Esau, but Esau is the older of the two.

Now, Esau was a good cook. He knew exactly how his dad liked his meat stew, so he'd often go out into the fields, make a kill, and then return to prepare his father's favorite meal. Esau was the brother with the hairy arms.

This day, Isaac requests that Esau prepare his favorite stew, with the promise that he'll give Esau his blessing and inheritance before he dies.

While the older boy leaves to go hunting, Rebekah puts her plan into action. For Jacob to receive Esau's blessing, he must act quickly. To do that, she tells Jacob to get Isaac's meat from their own goats. That done, to complete the ruse, they wrap Jacob's arms with hairy goatskin.

After Jacob receives Isaac's blessing, you can almost hear the hoofbeats of Esau's horse coming home from the hunt. Isaac had probably no more than said "Amen," when into the room strides Esau with the ingredients for his father's stew.

When the deception is revealed to one and all, Isaac delivers the implications of what has happened. Instead of a blessing for Esau, he now offers something far less desirable.

Isaac answers Esau's desperate pleas for blessing with, "You will live by the sword and you will serve your brother. But when you grow restless, you will throw his yoke from off your neck" (Genesis 27:40 NIV).

Despite the fact that Esau would hold a grudge against Jacob, there would be a happy ending. Against all odds, Jacob and Esau, years later, would be reunited, after much warring and unhappiness.

A Son's Hairy Tale

Think It Over

So how does this "hair-raising" tale relate to a contemporary father and his progeny? Consider: "All scripture is given by inspiration of God, and is profitable for doctrine, for reproof, for correction, for instruction in righteousness: that the man of God may be perfect, thoroughly furnished unto all good works" (2 Timothy 3:16–17).

As a dad, it's easy to play favorites. Do your children sense that one of them is more important to you than the other? Is there a Rebekah in the family circle? Read Psalm 106:4–5.

In the eyes of your children, are you and your wife of the same mind when it comes to raising them?

One could believe that most of the Bible fathers were rather aloof toward their children except when a dire emergency brought them close. Do you bond together just when times are tough, or do you make an effort to spend quality time with your kids every day?

For I was my father's son, tender and only beloved in the sight of my mother. He taught me also, and said unto me, Let thine heart retain my words: keep my commandments, and live.
PROVERBS 4:3–4

9. Father of the Brides
Scripture from Genesis 29–31

[Jacob began a journey east to Haran, where he was given employment by his uncle Laban, father of Rachel and Leah, and he lived under their roof.] And Laban said to him, Surely thou art my bone and my flesh. And he abode with him the space of a month.

And Laban said unto Jacob, Because thou art my brother, shouldest thou therefore serve me for nought? tell me, what shall thy wages be? And Laban had two daughters: the name of the elder was Leah, and the name of the younger was Rachel.

Leah was tender eyed; but Rachel was beautiful and well favoured. And Jacob loved Rachel; and said, I will serve thee seven years for Rachel thy younger daughter.

And Laban said, It is better that I give her to thee, than that I should give her to another man: abide with me.

And Jacob served seven years for Rachel; and they seemed unto him but a few days, for the love he had to her.

And Jacob said unto Laban, Give me my wife, for my days are fulfilled, that I may go in unto her. And Laban gathered together all the men of the place, and made a feast.

And it came to pass in the evening, that he took Leah his daughter, and brought her to him; and he went in unto her. And Laban gave unto his daughter Leah Zilpah his maid for an handmaid. And it came to pass, that in the morning, behold, it was Leah: and he said to Laban, What is this thou hast done unto me? did not I serve with thee for Rachel? wherefore then hast thou beguiled me?

And Laban said, It must not be so done in our country, to give the younger before the firstborn. Fulfil her week, and we will give thee this also for the service which thou shalt serve with me yet seven other years.

And Jacob did so, and fulfilled her week: and he gave him Rachel his daughter to wife also. And Laban gave to Rachel his daughter Bilhah his handmaid to be her maid.

And he went in also unto Rachel, and he loved also Rachel more than Leah, and served with him yet seven other years.

And when the LORD saw that Leah was hated, he opened her womb: but Rachel was barren. And Leah conceived, and bare a son, and she called his name Reuben: for she said, Surely the LORD hath looked upon my affliction; now therefore my husband will love me. . . .

And when Rachel saw that she bare Jacob no children, Rachel envied her sister; and said unto Jacob, Give me children, or else I die.

[Because Rachel is unable to conceive, she gives Jacob her maidservant, who bears Dan. Between Leah and the maidservants, ten sons and a daughter are born to Jacob.]

And God remembered Rachel, and God hearkened to her, and opened her womb. And she conceived, and bare a son; and said, God hath taken away my reproach: And she called his name Joseph.

Father of the Brides
The Story of Laban and Leah and Rachel

When it comes to miserable fathers-in-laws, Laban must take the cake. When it comes to daughters, Leah and Rachel would do well in a Jane Austen novel. And when you're thinking about gullible sons-in-law, Jacob should be right up there with the best of them.

There is more than one way to interpret Laban's relationship with his daughters.

1. Laban is holding onto his daughters as indentured servants, there being no Mrs. Laban around. After all, daughters have a way of pampering, or acquiescing to, their old dads.
2. Laban wants to be selective in choosing husbands for them—especially for Rachel, the beauty queen. There could be good money in such dealings.
3. Laban just may love his daughters so much that he believes no man is worthy of them—again, especially Rachel. Even that point of view has a basis in self-centeredness, a quality Laban possessed in spades.

How does one describe the special affection a dad has for a daughter? Such a connection is clearly a blessing from God. When a dad in the delivery room hears the words, "It's a girl," something in him goes tender inside. All thoughts of playing catch in the backyard or tinkering with an engine in the garage, activities perhaps anticipated with a son, disappear. You just want to hold this little girl and protect her—and she'll look up to you as her hero, for a while, anyway.

Did Laban acknowledge these feelings as a father? We'll never know. To an outsider looking in, Laban can be faulted for putting his own needs before those of his daughters. One commentary observes, "On the surface it appears that Laban used his daughters as bait, to get free labor out of Jacob."

(Before totally castigating Laban, recall that Jacob was a bit of a trickster himself. We know that Jacob beat hairy Esau out of his birthright by covering his arms with animal skin to fool his father, blind old Isaac.)

One cannot accuse the Old Testament writers of skirting "people" issues. They dealt with the practical issues of B.C. life, issues that still plague us in the twenty-first century. In a way, Laban's story sounds like something out of a celebrity tabloid, except that it's true! Consider that the Bible isn't afraid to include references to Jacob "lying with" Leah, or Rachel, or one of the servant women, or telling the reader that Jacob was attracted to Rachel because of her physical attributes (Genesis 29:17). Though often hidden by biblical language, even the most intimate acts of human life are worthy for inclusion in scripture.

Like the links of a chain, all of these patriarchal stories provide the reader with a sense of continuity that runs from Genesis through Revelation. Here, thanks to Leah and Rachel, we discover the leaders of the twelve tribes of Israel, who were all the sons of Jacob and Leah, Rachel, and their handmaidens. And, of course, we are introduced to Rachel's son Joseph, who was to be a foreshadowing of Jesus Christ.

Father of the Brides
Think It Over

Be sure to read the complete story of Laban and Jacob (and Leah and Rachel). It's a lengthy assignment, but worthwhile. The father-daughter/father-son theme is very nearly overwhelming, what with Laban and his two daughters and Jacob, the father of the twelve tribes of Israel. Is there a twenty-first-century example of such a far-reaching view of fatherhood?

How did you respond to Laban's use of his daughters to fulfill his own ends? If this happened today (in a modern form), what would be the end result for Laban?

Did Jacob get what he deserved? Why did God select a man like Jacob to bring forth the twelve tribes of Israel? Why did God select you to father the kids under your care?

Consider how great is the act of forgiveness—and its presence in this epic story. (Read Genesis 33 to see the reconciliation through forgiveness of Jacob and Esau.) Then read Mark 11:25–26.

Let all bitterness, and wrath, and anger, and clamour, and evil speaking, be put away from you, with all malice: and be ye kind one to another, tenderhearted, forgiving one another, even as God for Christ's sake hath forgiven you.
EPHESIANS 4:31–32

10. Trouble in the Family
Scripture from Genesis 34–35

And Dinah the daughter of Leah, which she bare unto Jacob, went out to see the daughters of the land. And when Shechem the son of Hamor the Hivite, prince of the country, saw her, he took her, and lay with her, and defiled her. And his soul clave unto Dinah the daughter of Jacob, and he loved the damsel, and spake kindly unto the damsel. And Shechem spake unto his father Hamor, saying, Get me this damsel to wife.

And Jacob heard that he had defiled Dinah his daughter: now his sons were with his cattle in the field: and Jacob held his peace until they were come.

And Hamor the father of Shechem went out unto Jacob to commune with him.

And the sons of Jacob came out of the field when they heard it: and the men were grieved, and they were very wroth, because he had wrought folly in Israel in lying with Jacob's daughter: which thing ought not to be done.

And Hamor communed with them, saying, The soul of my son Shechem longeth for your daughter: I pray you give her him to wife. . . . Let me find grace in your eyes, and what ye shall say unto me I will give. Ask me never so much dowry and gift, and I will give according as ye shall say unto me: but give me the damsel to wife.

And the sons of Jacob answered Shechem and Hamor his father deceitfully. . . . We cannot do this thing, to give our sister to one that is uncircumcised; for that were a reproach unto us: But in this will we consent unto you: If ye will be as we be, that every male of you be circumcised; then will we give our daughters unto you, and we will take your daughters to us, and we will dwell with you. . . . But if ye will not hearken unto us, to be circumcised; then will we take our daughter, and we will be gone. . . . And it came to pass on the third day, when they were sore, that two of the sons of Jacob, Simeon and Levi, Dinah's brethren, took each man his sword, and came upon the city boldly, and slew all the males. And they slew Hamor and Shechem his son with the edge of the sword, and took Dinah out of Shechem's house, and went out. The sons of Jacob. . .[looted] the city, because they had defiled their sister. . . . And Jacob said to Simeon and Levi, Ye have troubled me to make me to stink among the inhabitants of the land, among the Canaanites and the Perizzites: and I being few in number, they shall gather themselves together against me, and slay me; and I shall be destroyed, I and my house.

And they said, Should he deal with our sister as with an harlot?

And God said unto Jacob, Arise, go up to Bethel, and dwell there: and make there an altar unto God, that appeared unto thee when thou fleddest from the face of Esau thy brother.

Trouble in the Family
The Story of Jacob and Dinah

Twenty years after Jacob arrived at the home of his uncle, Laban, in Haran, Jacob decided to return to Canaan (Genesis 31–33) with all his family and possessions. It seemed best to make the departure when Laban was away. But Laban quickly discovered what happened, and he took out after Jacob to reclaim his property. The two tricksters finally resolved to go their separate ways by making peace with one another through a covenant at Mizpah.

Jacob and his crew journeyed on and finally arrived in the land of Canaan, settling in the city of Shalem. This then becomes the setting for the great shame of Jacob's life.

Commentators agree that Jacob was probably disappointed when Dinah was born. First, Leah, the wife with weak eyes, and not Rachel, the beautiful one, was Dinah's mother. Second, fathers needed all the strength and endurance necessary to work a sheep ranch, and Dinah could not provide that.

One can imagine Dinah's situation as the single daughter amid twelve brothers. While her brothers were protective of her, they wouldn't want to converse with her about stuff like clothes and boys. Likely, Leah was pretty busy running the household and didn't have too much time for her either.

As Dinah matured, she became a beautiful young woman, a woman who would be noticed when she went into Shalem. Perhaps it was on one of those trips that she met Shechem, regarded as local royalty. Responding like a spoiled nobleman, he decided to take what he wanted, and he wanted Dinah.

Meanwhile back at the ranch, Jacob was asking Leah, "Where is that daughter of yours?"

To which Leah responded, "Mine, why does she suddenly become 'mine' and not 'ours'?"

The problem very soon would become theirs. When Jacob and his sons found out that their sister had been raped, they reacted as you might expect—they were furious! But then they developed a plan.

And when Shechem's father, Hamor, came requesting Dinah's hand in marriage for Shechem, the brothers played perfect gentlemen in accepting Hamor's offer to make his land and its women theirs. Their only requirement? Jacob's sons insisted that all the men in Hamor and Shechem's land would have to be circumcised before they could enjoy their spoils. Hamor readily agreed.

While Hamor and his men were recovering from the circumcision, Jacob's sons slaughtered every male in the city, including Hamor and Shechem.

When Jacob learned of the massacre, however, at God's direction, he announced to the family they must flee the country and return to Bethel, where he then built an altar to God.

To contemporary fathers, the slaughter by Jacob's sons seems extreme, to put it mildly. But after the act was accomplished, Jacob responded to God, following His lead and seeking His forgiveness.

Trouble in the Family

Think It Over

Peruse Genesis 34. It's rough reading, even for Old Testament murder and mayhem. Did the punishment by Jacob's sons fit the crime?

The brothers' anger is certainly understandable, but taking it to that degree is unconscionable by today's standards. Are there times when our method of disciplining gets out of hand? Do we seek vindication more than discipline?

A young woman's attitude about men often depends upon her relationship with her dad. What qualities have you modeled that she might look for in a future spouse? How about sitting with a daughter and discussing this issue?

How does the Christian family prepare a daughter for trouble she may face in the world? This is a heavy topic, but it's not Mom's job alone to discuss it.

I will teach you the good and the right way.
1 SAMUEL 12:23

11. When Kids Disappoint
Scripture from Genesis 35, 37

Now the sons of Jacob were twelve: The sons of Leah; Reuben, Jacob's firstborn, and Simeon, and Levi, and Judah, and Issachar, and Zebulun: the sons of Rachel; Joseph, and Benjamin: and the sons of Bilhah, Rachel's handmaid; Dan, and Naphtali: and the sons of Zilpah, Leah's handmaid: Gad, and Asher. . . .

And Jacob dwelt in the land wherein his father was a stranger, in the land of Canaan.

These are the generations of Jacob. Joseph, being seventeen years old, was feeding the flock with his brethren. . .and Joseph brought unto his father their evil report.

Now Israel [Jacob] loved Joseph more than all his children, because he was the son of his old age: and he made him a coat of many colours. And when his brethren saw that their father loved him more than all his brethren, they hated him, and could not speak peaceably unto him.

And Joseph dreamed a dream, and he told it his brethren: and they hated him yet the more. And he said unto them, Hear, I pray you, this dream which I have dreamed: For, behold, we were binding sheaves in the field, and, lo, my sheaf arose, and also stood upright; and, behold, your sheaves stood round about, and made obeisance to my sheaf. . . .

And he dreamed yet another dream, and told it his brethren, and said, Behold, I have dreamed a dream more; and behold, the sun and the moon and the eleven stars made obeisance to me. . . .

And his brethren envied him; but his father observed the saying.

And his brethren went to feed their father's flock in Shechem. And Israel [Jacob] said unto Joseph, Do not thy brethren feed the flock in Shechem? Come, and I will send thee unto them. . . .

And Joseph went after his brethren, and found them in Dothan. And when they saw him afar off, even before he came near unto them, they conspired against him to slay him. And they said one to another, Behold, this dreamer cometh. Come now therefore, and let us slay him, and cast him into some pit, and we will say, Some evil beast hath devoured him: and we shall see what will become of his dreams.

And Reuben heard it, and he delivered him out of their hands; and said, Let us not kill him. . . . And it came to pass, when Joseph was come unto his brethren, that they stript Joseph out of his coat, his coat of many colours that was on him; and they took him, and cast him into a pit; and the pit was empty, there was no water in it.

And they sat down to eat bread: and they lifted up their eyes and looked, and, behold, a company of Ishmeelites came from Gilead with their camels bearing spicery and balm and myrrh, going to carry it down to Egypt.

And Judah said unto his brethren, What profit is it if we slay our brother, and conceal his blood? Come, and let us sell him to the Ishmeelites, and let not our hand be upon him; for he is our brother and our flesh. And his brethren were content….and they drew and lifted up Joseph out of the pit, and sold Joseph to the Ishmeelites for twenty pieces of silver: and they brought Joseph into Egypt. . . .

And they took Joseph's coat, and killed a kid of the goats, and dipped the coat in the blood; and they sent the coat of many colours, and they brought it to their father; and said, This have we found: know now whether it be thy son's coat or no.

And [Jacob] knew it, and said, It is my son's coat; an evil beast hath devoured him; Joseph is without doubt rent in pieces. And Jacob rent his clothes, and put sackcloth upon his loins, and mourned for his son many days. And all his sons and all his daughters rose up to comfort him; but he refused to be comforted; . . .thus his father wept for him.

And the Midianites sold [Joseph] into Egypt unto Potiphar, an officer of Pharaoh's, and captain of the guard.

When Kids Disappoint
The Story of Jacob and His Sons

No, the twelve sons and unknown number of daughters who called Jacob *father* did not all come from the same mother. There were four women involved: Leah, Leah's servant, Rachel, and Rachel's servant.

Rachel's sons were Benjamin and Joseph. Both boys were unusually close to their father, but Joseph was Jacob's favorite because he was born in Jacob's old age and Rachel was his mother. There was no way of hiding it: Joseph was Jacob's favorite, and his brothers hated him for it.

When Jacob presented Joseph with a richly ornamental robe, a coat of many colors, the brothers' jealousy reached a new level.

It's difficult to believe that brothers could be so hateful over something as insignificant as a colorful coat—that is, until Joseph started telling them about his dreams.

- Joseph's Dream No. 1: "We were binding sheaves of wheat, when suddenly my sheaf rose and stood, while yours bowed down to it!"
- Joseph's Dream No. 2: "The sun and the moon and eleven stars were bowing down to me!"

It didn't take Sigmund Freud to figure out what Joseph's dreams meant. Even the densest brother would get the message—their kid brother thought he was better than they. Moreover, even Jacob was chagrined by Joseph's boldness.

When there are jealous children in the family, it's the parents' responsibility to rectify the situation. Such was not the case with Jacob and his reprobate sons. Instead, the boys took matters into their own hands. They roughed up Joseph, stripped him of his clothes, and threw him into a dry well. When an Ishmaelite caravan came by, the brothers sold Joseph like a slave for twenty pieces of silver.

To make Joseph's disappearance seem like an accident, the brothers killed an animal and smeared its blood on the coat of many colors, which they then took to Jacob as proof of Joseph's violent demise.

Jacob's sons didn't commit murder. They only wanted to get rid of what they thought was a bratty kid brother. But their thoughtless behavior momentarily killed a father's happiness and destroyed, or so they thought, their brother's dreams.

But all was not lost: "And the Midianites sold him into Egypt unto Potiphar, an officer of Pharaoh's, and captain of the guard" (Genesis 37:36).

When Kids Disappoint

Think It Over

The story of Jacob and his boys is fraught with problems. In its biblical dimensions, it is overwhelming, but reduced to the size of your family, what does this epic of jealousy unleashed have to say about fatherhood?

While Jacob might never be voted "Father of the Year," how do you think he approached discipline? How did his wives influence him? Read Genesis 37:3. Is there truth in there for you?

Jealousy takes on a variety of traits between siblings, siblings and parents, and husbands and wives. Does your family demonstrate any traits of jealousy, and if so, what are they? Do you?

Consider this verse and then apply it to you and yours: "A sound heart is the life of the flesh: but envy the rottenness of the bones" (Proverbs 14:30). Open an opportunity for your gang to discuss it.

*Cause me to hear thy lovingkindness in the morning;
for in thee do I trust: cause me to know the way wherein I
should walk; for I lift up my soul unto thee.*
PSALM 143:8

12. When the Dream Comes to Pass
Scripture from Genesis 41–45, 50

[In Egypt, Joseph first worked as a slave for Potiphar but later was made manager over his entire household. Life was good—until Potiphar's wife tried to seduce Joseph and the young man refused her advances. Her false accusations of adultery, though, succeeded in sending Joseph to prison. While in prison, Joseph interpreted Pharaoh's dreams as indicating seven years of plenty followed by a terrible famine, which resulted in his release from prison and his promotion in the palace.]

And Pharaoh said unto Joseph, See, I have set thee over all the land of Egypt. . . . And Joseph was thirty years old when he stood before Pharaoh king of Egypt. . . .

Now when Jacob saw that there was corn in Egypt, Jacob said unto his sons, Why do ye look one upon another? . . . Get you down thither, and buy for us from thence; that we may live, and not die.

And Joseph's ten brethren went down to buy corn in Egypt. But Benjamin, Joseph's brother, Jacob sent not with his brethren; for he said, Lest peradventure mischief befall him. . . .

And Joseph was the governor over the land, and he it was that sold to all the people of the land: and Joseph's brethren came, and bowed down themselves before him with their faces to the earth. And Joseph saw his brethren, and he knew them, but made himself strange unto them, and spake roughly unto them; and he said unto them, Whence come ye? And they said, From the land of Canaan to buy food. . . .

And Joseph remembered the dreams which he

dreamed of them, and said unto them, Ye are spies; to see the nakedness of the land ye are come.

And they said unto him, Nay, my lord, but to buy food are thy servants come. We are all one man's sons, ... the sons of one man in the land of Canaan; and behold, the youngest is this day with our father, and one is not.

[Joseph continues to accuse them of spying, and holds them for three days.

Finally he sends them home to take grain to their household, but they must return with their youngest brother.]

And they said one to another, We are verily guilty concerning our brother, in that we saw the anguish of his soul, when he besought us, and we would not hear; therefore is this distress come upon us.

And Reuben answered them, saying, Spake I not unto you, saying, Do not sin against the child; and ye would not hear? Therefore, behold, also his blood is required. And they knew not that Joseph understood them; for he spake unto them by an interpreter.

And he turned himself about from them, and wept; . . .and took from them Simeon, and bound him before their eyes.

[Joseph's brothers return to their father in Canaan and tell him they must return to Egypt with Benjamin.]

And [Jacob] said, My son shall not go down with you; for his brother is dead, and he is left alone: if mischief befall him by the way in the which ye go, then shall ye bring down my gray hairs with sorrow to the grave.

[The family is soon out of supplies again, so Jacob tells his sons to return to Egypt to buy more. They convince Jacob that Benjamin must go with them and then return to Egypt. Joseph provides a lavish dinner and generous supplies for them and sends them on their way home. However, Joseph calls them back and accuses them of stealing from him. In the turmoil of this scene, Joseph finally reveals his identity to his brothers.]

And [Joseph] wept aloud: and the Egyptians and the house of Pharaoh heard. And Joseph said unto his brethren, I am Joseph; doth my father yet live? And his brethren could not answer him; for they were troubled at his presence. And Joseph said unto his brethren, Come near to me, I pray you. And they came near. And he said, I am Joseph your brother, whom ye sold into Egypt. . . . Haste ye, and go up to my father.

[Joseph is reunited with his father and brothers and moves their entire family to the land of Goshen. Upon Jacob's death, however, his brothers fear a final retribution. Joseph speaks to his brothers.]

But as for you, ye thought evil against me; but God meant it unto good, to bring to pass, as it is this day, to save much people alive.

When the Dream Comes to Pass
The Story of Jacob and Joseph

At the close of Act I, father Jacob is bereft of his loving son Joseph, to whom he had given a glorious coat that made his other sons jealous.

Act II opens in Potiphar's house with the Egyptian official's treacherous wife making false accusations about the young Joseph's behavior toward her. Because of Joseph's refusal to go to bed with her, Potiphar's wife flies into a jealous rage, resulting in Joseph's imprisonment.

It was that imprisonment, though, that opened the door for Joseph's lofty position under Pharaoh, the king of Egypt, providing grain to neighboring regions during a time of great famine. In ways known only to God, Joseph's Egyptian sojourn resulted in reconciliation with his brothers and the reuniting of himself with his beloved father.

After the reconciliation, Jacob lived in Egypt seventeen years. When Jacob was 147 years old, he made a final request that his bones not be buried in Egypt but in Canaan. Surprisingly, after Jacob's death, Pharaoh agreed, and Joseph was allowed to leave Egypt with his father's remains—accompanied by a full retinue of Pharaoh's servants.

Before Jacob's death, Joseph took his two Egypt-born boys, Manasseh and Ephraim, to say good-bye to their grandfather.

According to tradition, Jacob blessed each of his sons (Genesis 49:2–28). In his blessing for Joseph, Jacob explained, "The blessings of thy father have prevailed above the blessings of my progenitors unto the utmost bound of the everlasting hills: they shall be on the head of Joseph, and on the crown of the head of him that was separate from his brethren" (Genesis 49:26).

When the moment seemed right, Joseph addressed his brothers. To paraphrase, he said, "Don't be afraid. Those many years ago, what you intended to be harmful, God intended for good." Even anger and jealousy can "work together for good," according to God's plan.

Joseph's relationship with Jacob is unique in Old Testament history. No other man showed the same degree of tenderness and concern for an aging parent as did Joseph. When he gained his position in Egypt, no doubt he figured how it could help his father. When famine wiped out Jacob's resources, it seemed to have thrilled Joseph to care for his father as he did.

From Joseph's story, we can glean two lessons. The first concerns the destructive power of jealousy. Read the following scriptures: Deuteronomy 4:23–24; Proverbs 14:30; Proverbs 23:17; Song of Solomon 8:6; and 1 Corinthians 13:4–7.

The second lesson points out the need for adult children to take time for aging parents. To paraphrase scripture, be devoted to one another in family love. . .honor one another above yourselves. . .never be lacking in zeal. . . share with your aging parents who are in need. . .practice hospitality (see Romans 12:10–13).

Perhaps a third lesson is revealed in Genesis 50:21, when Joseph reassured his brothers that he would provide for them. True forgiveness involves giving some of yourself to those you are forgiving.

What this world needs are more Josephs!

When the Dream Comes to Pass

Think It Over

It is always thrilling to read how Joseph reconciled with his brothers. He cried so loudly that the Egyptians heard him, including Pharaoh's household!

Then, when Joseph had identified himself, he asked first about his beloved father. If you have a father/parent living, make contact with that loved one. Mend any problems, share remembrances, speak lovingly, write meaningful cards.

Joseph's story needs to be expressed in contemporary terms. For example, consider Potiphar's wife. Through time she has come in many guises—today, she is surely tempting young men via the Internet. If this is a problem in your life, pray about sharing your struggle with your spouse or a trusted friend. If you have teenaged boys in your family, talk to them about this area of temptation.

What other modern applications can be made from Joseph's story? Consider family relationships. What do your kids think of their aunts and uncles? Have their attitudes been formed by your relationship or your wife's relationship with your/her siblings? How can you improve your relationship with your siblings?

For I know the thoughts that I think toward you,
saith the LORD, thoughts of peace, and not of evil,
to give you an expected end.
JEREMIAH 29:11

13. The Boss Is My Father-in-Law
Scripture from Exodus 3–4

Now Moses kept the flock of Jethro his father in law, the priest of Midian: and he led the flock to the backside of the desert, and came to the mountain of God, even to Horeb.

And the angel of the LORD appeared unto him in a flame of fire out of the midst of a bush: and he looked, and, behold, the bush burned with fire, and the bush was not consumed. And Moses said, I will now turn aside, and see this great sight, why the bush is not burnt.

And when the LORD saw that he turned aside to see, God called unto him out of the midst of the bush, and said, Moses, Moses. And he said, Here am I. And he said, Draw not nigh hither: put off thy shoes from off thy feet, for the place whereon thou standest is holy ground. . . .

Now therefore, behold, the cry of the children of Israel is come unto me: and I have also seen the oppression wherewith the Egyptians oppress them. Come now therefore, and I will send thee unto Pharaoh, that thou mayest bring forth my people the children of Israel out of Egypt.

And Moses said unto God, Who am I, that I should go unto Pharaoh, and that I should bring forth the children of Israel out of Egypt? . . .

And the LORD said unto him, What is that in thine hand? And he said, A rod. And he said, Cast it on the ground. And he cast it on the ground, and it became a serpent; and Moses fled from before it. And the LORD said unto Moses, Put forth thine hand, and take it by the tail. And he put forth his hand, and caught it, and it became a rod in his hand:

That they may believe that the LORD God of their fathers, the God of Abraham, the God of Isaac, and the God of Jacob, hath appeared unto thee.

[Then Moses' hand became leprous until God healed it.]

And Moses said unto the LORD, O my LORD, I am not eloquent, neither heretofore, nor since thou hast spoken unto thy servant: but I am slow of speech, and of a slow tongue.

And the LORD said unto him, Who hath made man's mouth? or who maketh the dumb, or deaf, or the seeing, or the blind? have not I the LORD? . . .

And the anger of the LORD was kindled against Moses, and he said, Is not Aaron the Levite thy brother? I know that he can speak well. And also, behold, he cometh forth to meet thee: and when he seeth thee, he will be glad in his heart. And thou shalt speak unto him, and put words in his mouth: and I will be with thy mouth, and with his mouth, and will teach you what ye shall do.

And he shall be thy spokesman unto the people: and he shall be, even he shall be to thee instead of a mouth, and thou shalt be to him instead of God. And thou shalt take this rod in thine hand, wherewith thou shalt do signs.

And Moses went and returned to Jethro his father in law, and said unto him, Let me go, I pray thee, and return unto my brethren which are in Egypt, and see whether they be yet alive. And Jethro said to Moses, Go in peace. . . .

And Moses took his wife and his sons, and set them upon an ass, and he returned to the land of Egypt: and Moses took the rod of God in his hand.

The Boss Is My Father-in-Law
The Story of Jethro and Moses

Moses' family tree as given in Exodus 6 indicates his father's name was Amram (grandson of Levi) and his mother, Jochebed (who was her husband's aunt). Moses had a sister Miriam (who became a prophetess), and a brother, Aaron (who became Moses' spokesperson before Pharaoh).

We don't know what influence Amram had on his son, but Jochebed's role is impressive. It was she who saved baby Moses from certain death by sending him down the Nile in a basket, to escape Pharaoh's edict that all Hebrew male babies be killed. And it was Miriam who witnessed Pharaoh's daughter rescue Moses and then helped Jochebed be "hired" as his nurse.

Raised as an Egyptian, Moses nonetheless carried a love for his own people in his heart. When he saw an Egyptian mistreating a Hebrew, Moses killed the offending Egyptian and then escaped to Midian. That's where he met his father-in-law-to-be, a priest named Jethro.

Now Jethro had seven daughters, who just happened to come over to the village well at the same time Moses was there washing up after his escape from Egypt. While the girls poured water for their flock, a rough bunch of shepherds came by and started harassing them. Moses ran off the rough shepherds and watered the sisters' flock for them. He was a charmer.

As the Lord would have it, Moses became a favorite in Jethro's home, and he was offered one of the priest's daughters, Zipporah, in exchange for being handy with his sheep.

On a day that was probably as ordinary as any, Moses grabbed his staff and set out for a day with Jethro's sheep, little suspecting that he'd have a God event that would change his life forever.

This was "Burning Bush Day," when God spoke to Moses about getting the children of Israel out of Egypt. It's also the time when Moses tried to change God's mind—in effect, to use his brother Aaron as Moses' mouthpiece. Finally, this was the day the Lord gave Moses signs of His power, and Moses surrendered to God's plan.

From this vantage point, we see how God brought Jethro and his family into Moses' life for His purposes. We see how the rude shepherds at the well contributed to God's plan, as well as Moses' hasty escape from Egypt.

Don't minimize Jethro in God's master plan for Moses and the Israelites in Egypt. The Lord uses fathers-in-law. They are usually able to look at their child's mate through objective eyes, and with less concern about family history.

The Boss Is My Father-in-Law

Think It Over

Not all of us have fathers who contribute positively to our lives. If Moses didn't have that as a child, his father-in-law Jethro made up for it in his adulthood. In what ways can you make a contribution to one who is without parental guidance? Apply Colossians 3:16.

Think about God's will for your life. Pray about Proverbs 16:9: "A man's heart deviseth his way: but the LORD directeth his steps." What's the difference between course devising and step directing?

Do you believe Hebrews 10:36? "For ye have need of patience, that, after ye have done the will of God, ye might receive the promise." What has God promised you?

Before you can be a person of influence, read Hebrews 13:20–21 a number of times and then pray over the words. Consider the following:

1) How much do I want to be "perfect" [complete] in my works?
2) How am I seeking His will?
3) How "well pleasing" am I in His sight?

And be not conformed to this world: but be ye transformed by the renewing of your mind, that ye may prove what is that good, and acceptable, and perfect, will of God.
ROMANS 12:2

14. A Father's Tragic Vow

Scripture from Judges 10–11

And the children of Israel did evil again in the sight of the LORD. . . .

And the anger of the LORD was hot against Israel, and he sold them into the hands of the Philistines, and into the hands of the children of Ammon. . . .

And the children of Israel said unto the LORD, We have sinned: do thou unto us whatsoever seemeth good unto thee; deliver us only, we pray thee, this day. And they put away the strange gods from among them, and served the LORD: and his soul was grieved for the misery of Israel. . . .

Now Jephthah the Gileadite was a mighty man of valour. . . . And it came to pass in process of time, that the children of Ammon made war against Israel. And it was so, that when the children of Ammon made war against Israel, the elders of Gilead went to fetch Jephthah out of the land of Tob: And they said unto Jephthah, Come, and be our captain, that we may fight with the children of Ammon. . . .

And Jephthah said unto the elders of Gilead, If ye bring me home again to fight against the children of Ammon, and the LORD deliver them before me, shall I be your head? And the elders of Gilead said unto Jephthah, The LORD be witness between us, if we do not so according to thy words. . . .

Then the Spirit of the LORD came upon Jephthah, and he passed over Gilead, and Manasseh, and passed over Mizpeh of Gilead, and from Mizpeh of Gilead he passed over unto the children of Ammon. And Jephthah vowed a vow unto the LORD, and said, If thou shalt without fail deliver the children of Ammon into mine hands, then it shall be, that whatsoever cometh forth of the doors of my house to meet me, when I return in peace from the children of Ammon, shall surely be the LORD's, and I will offer it up for a burnt offering.

So Jephthah passed over unto the children of Ammon to fight against them; and the LORD delivered them into his hands. . . .

And Jephthah came to Mizpeh unto his house, and, behold, his daughter came out to meet him with timbrels and with dances: and she was his only child; beside her he had neither son nor daughter.

And it came to pass, when he saw her, that he rent his clothes, and said, Alas, my daughter! thou hast brought me very low, and thou art one of them that trouble me: for I have opened my mouth unto the LORD, and I cannot go back.

And she said unto him, My father, if thou hast opened thy mouth unto the LORD, do to me according to that which hath proceeded out of thy mouth; forasmuch as the LORD hath taken vengeance for thee of thine enemies, even of the children of Ammon. And she said unto her father, Let this thing be done for me: let me alone two months, that I may go up and down upon the mountains, and bewail my virginity, I and my fellows. And he said, Go. And he sent her away for two months: and she went with her companions, and bewailed her virginity upon the mountains.

And it came to pass at the end of two months, that she returned unto her father, who did with her according to his vow which he had vowed.

A Father's Tragic Vow
The Story of Jephthah and His Daughter

This crisis is unimaginable to any contemporary father who has the dearest memories of his little girl. From the first second you saw her in her mother's arms, still damp from delivery, to her first day of school leaving the house a bundle of worry (and returning with a head full of excitement), to her sitting beside her beau at your Sunday table and reading your eyes for signs that you approve—you knew she was God's gift to you and her mother.

Then there is Jephthah! Bible teachers don't agree on the purpose of this story. Language experts say that the word for sacrifice used here meant "burnt offering." But human sacrifice was strictly forbidden by Mosaic law and is repugnant to God.

How then could Jephthah believe he could curry favor with God by offering Him a human sacrifice?

One commentator argues that God allows people to make wrong choices, even while He works out His higher good. One less than conservative interpretation of this event is to recognize that Jephthah used the Hebrew word *olah* (sacrifice) in a figurative sense. That is, he said it as we might say, "Sure I can sacrifice five bucks to help send a kid to summer camp."

Still others would have us believe that Jephthah's sacrifice was accepting his daughter's virginity, and denying himself the joy of extending his family.

Those who, with great bewilderment, accept the story as written, make no excuses for the father's actions. Was he caught up in the excitement of battle? No doubt. Did he believe a sheep or goat would be first out the door to greet him? Most likely. By his actions, he was devastated when he saw his daughter.

This shocking story of Jephthah is another Old Testament example of what happens when someone does what they think is right in their own mind instead of consulting God first.

Dads, our words and actions have far-reaching results. And in a practical sense, our children often are the beneficiaries—or victims—of our language. Today as you interact with your family members, coworkers, and fellow church members, be aware of the impressions you are leaving in their minds.

Christian parents have a responsibility not to harm reputations or the good names of those who have different opinions. Some of us remember a mom who would kick us under the table and remark, "Little pitchers have big ears!"

A Father's Tragic Vow

Think About It

How did reading this Old Testament story first affect you? Because Jephthah's story is part of inspired scripture, it has a message for you. What might that message be? Let your wife or daughter read it. What is their reaction?

Remember this Bible verse: "Let the words of my mouth, and the meditation of my heart, be acceptable in thy sight, O LORD, my strength, and my redeemer" (Psalm 19:14).

Consider the verse of scripture that appears at the bottom of this page. To whom or to what have you submitted yourself? That necessitates your personal will—and that brings us back to Jephthah. God allowed Jephthah to make his own decisions—and then used him to bring about His will, which was a victory in battle. God has given us free will…but we need to seek His will before making any life-changing decisions.

Submit yourselves therefore to God.
Resist the devil, and he will flee from you.
JAMES 4:7

15. My Son Brought Down the House

Scripture from Judges 13

And there was a certain man of Zorah, of the family of the Danites, whose name was Manoah; and his wife was barren, and bare not. And the angel of the LORD appeared unto the woman, and said unto her, Behold now, thou art barren, and bearest not: but thou shalt conceive, and bear a son. Now therefore beware, I pray thee, and drink not wine nor strong drink, and eat not any unclean thing: For, lo, thou shalt conceive, and bear a son; and no razor shall come on his head: for the child shall be a Nazarite unto God from the womb: and he shall begin to deliver Israel out of the hand of the Philistines.

Then the woman came and told her husband. . . . Then Manoah intreated the LORD, and said, O my Lord, let the man of God which thou didst send come again unto us, and teach us what we shall do unto the child that shall be born.

And God hearkened to the voice of Manoah; and the angel of God came again unto the woman as she sat in the field: but Manoah her husband was not with her. And the woman made haste, and ran, and shewed her husband, and said unto him, Behold, the man hath appeared unto me, that came unto me the other day.

And Manoah arose, and went after his wife, and came to the man, and said unto him, Art thou the man that spakest unto the woman? And he said, I am.

And Manoah said, Now let thy words come to pass. How shall we order the child, and how shall we do unto him? And the angel of the LORD said unto Manoah, Of all that I said unto the woman let her beware. . . .

And Manoah said unto the angel of the LORD, I pray thee, let us detain thee, until we shall have made ready a kid for thee. And the angel of the LORD said unto Manoah, Though thou detain me, I will not eat of thy bread: and if thou wilt offer a burnt offering, thou must offer it unto the LORD. For Manoah knew not that he was an angel of the LORD. . . .

So Manoah took a kid with a meat offering, and offered it upon a rock unto the LORD: and the angel did wonderously; and Manoah and his wife looked on. For it came to pass, when the flame went up toward heaven from off the altar, that the angel of the LORD ascended in the flame of the altar. And Manoah and his wife looked on it, and fell on their faces to the ground.

But the angel of the LORD did no more appear to Manoah and to his wife. Then Manoah knew that he was an angel of the LORD. And Manoah said unto his wife, We shall surely die, because we have seen God.

But his wife said unto him, If the LORD were pleased to kill us, he would not have received a burnt offering and a meat offering at our hands, neither would he have shewed us all these things, nor would as at this time have told us such things as these.

And the woman bare a son, and called his name Samson: and the child grew, and the LORD blessed him.

My Son Brought Down the House
The Story of Manoah and Samson

The description of Manoah (soon to become Samson's father) in the thirteenth chapter of the book of Judges rings a bell of recognition for most husbands, and particularly husbands of pregnant women.

1. When a mother-to-be is put on a special diet, her husband must endure the same (verse 4).
2. Often dads disagree with moms about fancy hairdos on their sons—but this was not going to happen in Manoah's household. Per the angel's instructions, no one was to mess up Samson's hair (verse 5).
3. Manoah's pregnant wife is out working in the fields, while weary husband is stretched out on the ancient version of the couch (verses 10–11).
4. There would be no discussion about which church to raise the boy in—Samson was to be a Nazarite (verse 5).

That was then, this is now. Contrary to the best prenatal care, the adult Samson did not live up to his Nazarite vows (Judges 14). He paid no attention to dietary laws, he looked for love among Philistine women, and he turned his back on the God so venerated in his childhood home.

"Is there never a woman among the daughters of thy brethren, or among all my people, that thou goest to take a wife of the uncircumcised Philistines?" asked Manoah (Judges 14:3). Bible teachers sometimes explain Samson's involvement with the Philistines as an indication that God was using Samson as a spokesman to confront the Philistines.

As the whole world knows, another foolish Philistine romance, this time with Delilah, cost him his strength and sight.

With his arms outstretched, Samson's final words rang out, "O Lord God, remember me, I pray thee" (Judges 16:28). And Samson met his death—and caused the death of thousands of Philistines at the same time—by pulling down the pillars of the temple of Dagon.

Unfortunately, Manoah's name isn't mentioned again until after Samson's death. "Then his brethren and all the house of his father came down, and took him, and brought him up, and buried him between Zorah and Eshtaol in the buryingplace of Manoah his father" (Judges 16:31).

The writer of the New Testament book of Hebrews remembered Samson by including him in the listing of the faithful (Hebrews 11:32). Although Samson strayed, in the end he demonstrated that his strength came from the Lord. In his dying act he was faithful.

My Son Brought Down the House

Think It Over

Samson may be difficult to take seriously. Cartoons, movies, and even an opera have been made based on his life. But there's a reason he's in the Bible. As an early judge—the precursor to kings—Samson was used by God to influence His people. How does God influence you through other people? Think about your spouse, pastor, teacher, and close friends.

Before Samson's conception, an angel told his mother that he was to be a lifelong Nazarite (as opposed to taking the vow for a limited amount of time). Many promises are made at the birth of a child. Have you kept any that you made? Have you shared the promise with your child, regardless of his or her age?

Infatuations can be dangerous. Read Proverbs 13:20, at the bottom of this page. How does that relate to your relationships?

Everyone knows that Samson's great strength came from his uncut hair. Where does yours come from?

He that walketh with wise men shall be wise:
but a companion of fools shall be destroyed.
PROVERBS 13:20

16. Of Sheep and a King
Scripture from 1 Samuel 16–17

And the LORD said unto Samuel, How long wilt thou mourn for Saul, seeing I have rejected him from reigning over Israel? Fill thine horn with oil, and go, I will send thee to Jesse the Bethlehemite: for I have provided me a king among his sons.

And Samuel said, How can I go? if Saul hear it, he will kill me. And the LORD said, Take an heifer with thee, and say, I am come to sacrifice to the LORD. And call Jesse to the sacrifice, and I will shew thee what thou shalt do: and thou shalt anoint unto me him whom I name unto thee.

And Samuel did that which the LORD spake, and came to Bethlehem. And the elders of the town trembled at his coming, and said, Comest thou peaceably?

And he said, Peaceably: I am come to sacrifice unto the LORD: sanctify yourselves, and come with me to the sacrifice. And he sanctified Jesse and his sons, and called them to the sacrifice.

And it came to pass, when they were come, that he looked on Eliab, and said, Surely the LORD's anointed is before him.

But the LORD said unto Samuel, Look not on his countenance, or on the height of his stature; because I have refused him: for the LORD seeth not as man seeth; for man looketh on the outward appearance, but the LORD looketh on the heart. . . .

Again, Jesse made seven of his sons to pass before Samuel. And Samuel said unto Jesse, The LORD hath not chosen these.

And Samuel said unto Jesse, Are here all thy children?

And he said, There remaineth yet the youngest, and, behold, he keepeth the sheep. And Samuel said unto Jesse, Send and fetch him. . . . Now he was ruddy, and withal of a beautiful countenance, and goodly to look to. And the LORD said, Arise, anoint him: for this is he.

Then Samuel took the horn of oil, and anointed him in the midst of his brethren: and the Spirit of the LORD came upon David from that day forward. So Samuel rose up, and went to Ramah. . . .

And the three eldest sons of Jesse went and followed Saul to the battle: . . .But David went and returned from Saul to feed his father's sheep at Bethlehem.

And the Philistine drew near morning and evening, and presented himself forty days. . . .

And David said unto Saul, Let no man's heart fail because of him; thy servant will go and fight with this Philistine. . . .

And [David] took his staff in his hand, and chose him five smooth stones out of the brook, and put them in a shepherd's bag which he had, even in a scrip; and his sling was in his hand: and he drew near to the Philistine. . . .

And it came to pass, when the Philistine arose, and came, and drew nigh to meet David, that David hastened, and ran toward the army to meet the Philistine. And David put his hand in his bag, and took thence a stone, and slang it, and smote the Philistine in his forehead, that the stone sunk into his forehead; and he fell upon his face to the earth. . . . And when the Philistines saw their champion was dead, they fled. . . .

And Saul said to him, Whose son art thou, thou young man? And David answered, I am the son of thy servant Jesse the Bethlehemite.

Of Sheep and a King
The Story of Jesse and David

Imagine Jesse's curiosity when the prophet Samuel showed up at his front door asking to look over his sons. Seven of the boys were hanging around and the eighth was down in the pasture, probably playing his home-made harp, testing out a new song on his dad's sheep.

His golden voice might be singing, "The earth is the LORD's, and the fulness thereof; the world, and they that dwell therein" (Psalm 24:1), or "The LORD is my shepherd; I shall not want. He maketh me to lie down in green pastures: he leadeth me beside the still waters" (Psalm 23:1–2).

Back at the house, Samuel sized up the boys hanging around the living room, but he received no indication from the Lord which of them was to be Israel's next king.

Jesse responded to Samuel's request for more sons by acknowledging the youngest was in the pasture caring for the sheep. Maybe Jesse knew full well that David was out there making music. Samuel couldn't be interested in his youngest, the dreamer.

When David finally appeared, Samuel received the divine word that this son was the one.

Imagine David's bewilderment when he was asked to kneel and bow his head for the anointing. An amazed Jesse may have asked himself, "How come David?" And can't you imagine the subsequent conversations David had with his sheep?

Jesse had to have been proud of his boys. His eldest sons were fighting in King Saul's army against the

Philistines, and the youngest was obediently watching his flocks. When David, at Jesse's request, brought his brothers on the battlefield provisions from their father, his own fabled military career began. That's when David saw the giant Goliath.

Of course, when young David felled Goliath with a stone and slingshot, he caught the eye of King Saul, the very man he was anointed to replace.

The story of Jesse's boy David is overwhelming. There would be dark days ahead for the future king and during his reign: Saul would turn on him and attempt to kill him; people whom he loved would be taken from him; and he would morally cave in to lust and murder.

But let's not get ahead of ourselves. Why was David's anointing so significant? Because from his royal bloodline would come the Messiah (check out the genealogy in Matthew 1:1–17).

And in the sixth month the angel Gabriel was sent from God unto a city of Galilee, named Nazareth, to a virgin espoused to a man whose name was Joseph, of the house of David.
LUKE 1:26–27

And Joseph also went up from Galilee, out of the city of Nazareth, into Judaea, unto the city of David, which is called Bethlehem;(because he was of the house and lineage of David).
LUKE 2:4

Of Sheep and a King

Think It Over

It's tempting to read more into Jesse's seeming surprise when Samuel wished to interview his youngest son, David. What do you feel went through Jesse's mind at that moment? What are your dreams for your kids? Are they realistic? How are you preparing your children for their future?

As fathers, when we hold that baby in our arms, watch him or her on the basketball court, or listen to his or her piano recital, we have such dreams for them. At those moments, it's impossible to believe they won't succeed... or worse, that they would ever turn their backs on God. How are you doing as a spiritual role model? Now's a good time to read Psalm 51:10.

Got a kid in your family circle who's a little out of step with everyone else? Maybe "singing to the sheep"? How do you keep that child from living on the edge?

When the prophet Samuel barged in on Jesse's home with anointing oil, what do you think went through his sons' minds and hearts? Read 1 Peter 5:5–7 and write down your impressions.

Obey them that have the rule over you, and submit yourselves:
for they watch for your souls, as they that must give account,
that they may do it with joy, and not with grief:
for that is unprofitable for you.
HEBREWS 13:17

17. Dad, I Can't Share Your Values
Scripture from I Samuel 10, 16, 19–20

[David is brought into Saul's service.] And Saul said unto his servants, Provide me now a man that can play well, and bring him to me.

Then answered one of the servants, and said, Behold, I have seen a son of Jesse the Bethlehemite, that is cunning in playing, and a mighty valiant man, and a man of war, and prudent in matters, and a comely person, and the LORD is with him. . . .

And David came to Saul, and stood before him: and he loved him greatly; and he became his armourbearer. . . . And it came to pass, when the evil spirit from God was upon Saul, that David took an harp, and played with his hand: so Saul was refreshed, and was well, and the evil spirit departed from him.

[After the Philistine giant Goliath is killed by David, the crowds praise David, crying, "Saul hath slain his thousands, and David his ten thousands," and Saul becomes jealous.]

And Saul spake to Jonathan his son, and to all his servants, that they should kill David. But Jonathan Saul's son delighted much in David: and Jonathan told David, saying, Saul my father seeketh to kill thee: now therefore, I pray thee, take heed to thyself until the morning, and abide in a secret place, and hide thyself:

And Jonathan spake good of David unto Saul his father, and said unto him, Let not the king sin against his servant, against David; because he hath not sinned against thee, and because his works have been to theeward very good. . . .

Then Saul's anger was kindled against Jonathan, and he said unto him, Thou son of the perverse rebellious woman, do not I know that thou hast chosen the son of Jesse to thine own confusion, and unto the confusion of thy mother's nakedness?

For as long as the son of Jesse liveth upon the ground, thou shalt not be established, nor thy kingdom. Wherefore now send and fetch him unto me, for he shall surely die.

And Jonathan answered Saul his father, and said unto him, Wherefore shall he be slain? what hath he done? And Saul cast a javelin at him to smite him: whereby Jonathan knew that it was determined of his father to slay David. So Jonathan arose from the table in fierce anger, and did eat no meat the second day of the month: for he was grieved for David, because his father had done him shame.

And it came to pass in the morning, that Jonathan went out into the field at the time appointed with David. . . . David arose out of a place toward the south, and fell on his face to the ground, and bowed himself three times: and they kissed one another, and wept one with another, until David exceeded.

And Jonathan said to David, Go in peace, forasmuch as we have sworn both of us in the name of the LORD, saying, The LORD be between me and thee, and between my seed and thy seed for ever. And he arose and departed: and Jonathan went into the city.

Dad, I Can't Share Your Values
The Story of Saul and Jonathan

Jared, a teenager who lives in my condo complex, has a good friend named Ross who often sleeps over. According to Jared's mom, Ross seems to relish the experience of being in a Christian home, "with all the prayers and hugging that entails."

One morning as Ross pushed away from their breakfast table, he reported that he'd told his family he wanted to live like Jared's family. He was tired of all their bickering and mean ways.

Perhaps such was the case with Saul and his son Jonathan.

After David's defeat of Goliath, when he became a legend in Saul's army, the boys somehow became acquainted. Like all adolescents, they probably sized each other up, comparing themselves to each other. One was a son of privilege, the other a country boy who was good with animals and made up songs. Perhaps it was their common love of adventure that brought them together. David could tell Jonathan about his bouts with wild animals—like protecting his sheep from a bear—while the king's son might have had breathtaking tales about blood-drenched battles and narrow escapes with his father.

Did Jonathan ever spend nights at David's house? If he had, he would have experienced something new to him—a family that loved God and each other. He would have watched David's father Jesse offer prayers and go through the rituals of their faith. Perhaps, like Ross did with his family, he wanted to say to Saul, "Father, I cannot live this way. Your ways are not my ways."

But when the jealous King Saul commands Jonathan to kill David, there the modern-day comparison ends. We can imagine the conversation between the two friends went something like this:

"What's the big deal, Jonathan? How come you want to see me?"

"I asked you here to warn you!"

"About what?"

"My father, the king, wants you dead."

"But what do. . . ?"

"He wants me to kill you!"

The first and second books of Samuel record the tragic, downwardly spiraling relationship between Saul and David. Saul in his psychotic mindset continued to blame David for his failures—and he took it out on Jonathan.

But then came Saul's last battle on Mount Gilboa, where the Philistines evened the score for Goliath's death by killing the king's three sons—including Jonathan. In desperate sorrow Saul took his armor bearer's sword and killed himself.

And David? His words were recorded as follows: "I am distressed for thee, my brother Jonathan: very pleasant hast thou been unto me: thy love to me was wonderful, passing the love of women. How are the mighty fallen, and the weapons of war perished!" (2 Samuel 1:26–27).

Dad, I Can't Share Your Values

Think It Over

Like Shakespearean tragedies after it, the Saul/Jonathan/ David story packs a wallop. How can any father respond to this slice of biblical history without examining his own life and influence?

Ask yourself these questions: Do your kids recognize your value system? And if so, how does it affect them?

Whatever your vocation, how does what you do contribute other than financially to your family's well-being? Think about the ways your vocation affects the time you're able to spend with your family and your physical well-being, state of mind, and disposition.

What would happen if someone in your family circle said, "Dad, I can't share your values?" What would be your response?

Read Matthew 6:33 below. How does that verse speak to you?

But seek ye first the Kingdom of God, and his righteousness; and all those things shall be added unto you.
MATTHEW 6:33

18. Daddy, I Hardly Knew You

Scripture from 2 Samuel 4, 9

And Jonathan, Saul's son, had a son that was lame of his feet. He was five years old when the tidings came of Saul and Jonathan out of Jezreel, and his nurse took him up, and fled: and it came to pass, as she made haste to flee, that he fell, and became lame. And his name was Mephibosheth. [After David is crowned king, he asks for Mephibosheth.] And there was of the house of Saul a servant whose name was Ziba. And when they had called him unto David, the king said unto him, Art thou Ziba? And he said, Thy servant is he.

And the king said, Is there not yet any of the house of Saul, that I may shew the kindness of God unto him? And Ziba said unto the king, Jonathan hath yet a son, which is lame on his feet.

And the king said unto him, Where is he? And Ziba said unto the king, Behold, he is in the house of Machir, the son of Ammiel, in Lodebar.

Then king David sent, and fetched him out of the house of Machir, the son of Ammiel, from Lodebar.

Now when Mephibosheth, the son of Jonathan, the son of Saul, was come unto David, he fell on his face, and did reverence. And David said, Mephibosheth. And he answered, Behold thy servant!

And David said unto him, Fear not: for I will surely shew thee kindness for Jonathan thy father's sake, and will restore thee all the land of Saul thy father; and thou shalt eat bread at my table continually.

And he bowed himself, and said, What is thy servant,

that thou shouldest look upon such a dead dog as I am?

Then the king called to Ziba, Saul's servant, and said unto him, I have given unto thy master's son all that pertained to Saul and to all his house.

Thou therefore, and thy sons, and thy servants, shall till the land for him, and thou shalt bring in the fruits, that thy master's son may have food to eat: but Mephibosheth thy master's son shall eat bread alway at my table. Now Ziba had fifteen sons and twenty servants.

Then said Ziba unto the king, According to all that my lord the king hath commanded his servant, so shall thy servant do. As for Mephibosheth, said the king, he shall eat at my table, as one of the king's sons.

And Mephibosheth had a young son, whose name was Micha. And all that dwelt in the house of Ziba were servants unto Mephibosheth.

So Mephibosheth dwelt in Jerusalem: for he did eat continually at the king's table; and was lame on both his feet.

Daddy, I Hardly Knew You
The Story of Jonathan and Mephibosheth

If you can pronounce Jonathan's son's name, and then spell it, you're having a really good day. That said, the narrative of Jonathan and his crippled son reads almost like a Charles Dickens novel.

Of course, David is in the middle of this story. Perhaps if he weren't, we'd never have heard of Mephibosheth.

- Setting: David's palace; perhaps toward evening when thoughts of other days come to mind.
- Provocation: Recalling his friend Jonathan, son of King Saul.

No doubt King David shivers when he recalls how Jonathan saved his life from Saul's spear. Maybe David's mind then returns to those carefree days when he and Jonathan first became friends, two soldiers who came to be as close as brothers.

David undoubtedly remembers when the news came to him of Saul and Jonathan's death. At that time he had lamented, "How are the mighty fallen in the midst of the battle! O Jonathan, thou wast slain in thine high places. I am distressed for thee, my brother Jonathan: very pleasant hast thou been unto me: thy love to me was wonderful, passing the love of women. How are the mighty fallen, and the weapons of war perished!" (2 Samuel 1:25-27).

Coming back to the present, David calls for the chief steward of Saul's estate, Ziba, and asks if anyone still lives from the house of Saul. "I want to show him kindness for Jonathan's sake," David says. This is when David learns of Jonathan's son, Mephibosheth.

"Tell me about him," David asks.

"This son is named Mephibosheth. He was five years old when his father and grandfather were killed. His nurse secreted him out of the house, and ran to keep him safe. She fell with him in her arms and the boy became crippled as a result."

"Where is he now?"

"He is living with Makir in Lo Debar, on an estate far from here. Makir is a wealthy benefactor who has cared for Mephibosheth since Jonathan's death."

David then had Mephibosheth brought to Jerusalem from Lo Debar. One can imagine the anticipation and excitement David felt, awaiting the young man's appearance.

"Mephibosheth!"

"Your servant," he replied.

"Do not be afraid, Mephibosheth. I will show you kindness."

"But why?"

Then David related the boyhood tales of a young shepherd and his best friend, the king's son, Jonathan. And in great seriousness, David told of the promise he had made to the young man's father. "I will always care for your family."

So Mephibosheth sat at David's table for every meal, and all the land that had belonged to King Saul was his. King David was a man who kept his promises.

As for Jonathan, the Bible gives no indication of his parenting abilities, yet in the eyes of David, the young man he took in was fine, because Jonathan was his father.

Think It Over

The story of David's care of and provision for Mephibosheth is one of the most heartwarming in the Old Testament. Nothing required David to seek out and care for Jonathan's son—except the promise David had made to Jonathan. Prayerfully ask yourself, "Do I take my promises seriously? How about the ones I make to my children?"

Jesus expresses this need for compassion during what has come to be called the Olivet Discourse (see Matthew 25). To paraphrase, Jesus says that when we take in a stranger, care for the sick, and visit those in prison—in other words, helping "the least of these"—we are doing such acts for Him.

Are there any Mephibosheths who need you?

Is it not to deal thy bread to the hungry,
and that thou bring the poor that are cast out to thy house?
when thou seest the naked, that thou cover him;
and that thou hide not thyself from thine own flesh?
ISAIAH 58:7

19. When a Father's Heart Breaks

Scripture from 2 Samuel 15–18

[David's son Absalom conspires against his father, and leads a revolt against the king.] There came a messenger to David, saying, The hearts of the men of Israel are after Absalom.

And David said unto all his servants that were with him at Jerusalem, Arise, and let us flee; for we shall not else escape from Absalom: make speed to depart, lest he overtake us suddenly, and bring evil upon us, and smite the city with the edge of the sword. . . .

And Absalom met the servants of David. And Absalom rode upon a mule, and the mule went under the thick boughs of a great oak, and his head caught hold of the oak, and he was taken up between the heaven and the earth; and the mule that was under him went away.

And a certain man saw it, and told Joab, and said, Behold, I saw Absalom hanged in an oak. And Joab said unto the man that told him, And, behold, thou sawest him, and why didst thou not smite him there to the ground? and I would have given thee ten shekels of silver, and a girdle. And the man said unto Joab, Though I should receive a thousand shekels of silver in mine hand, yet would I not put forth mine hand against the king's son: for in our hearing the king charged thee and Abishai and Ittai, saying, Beware that none touch the young man Absalom. . . . Then said Joab, I may not tarry thus with thee. And he took three darts in his hand, and thrust them through the heart of Absalom, while he was yet alive in the midst of the oak. And ten young men that bare Joab's armour compassed about and smote

Absalom, and slew him. . . .

And they took Absalom, and cast him into a great pit in the wood, and laid a very great heap of stones upon him: and all Israel fled every one to his tent. . . .

Then said Ahimaaz the son of Zadok, Let me now run, and bear the king tidings, how that the LORD hath avenged him of his enemies.

And Joab said unto him, Thou shalt not bear tidings this day, but thou shalt bear tidings another day: but this day thou shalt bear no tidings, because the king's son is dead. Then said Joab to Cushi, Go tell the king what thou hast seen. And Cushi bowed himself unto Joab, and ran. . . .

And David sat between the two gates: and the watchman went up to the roof over the gate unto the wall, and lifted up his eyes, and looked, and behold a man running alone. And the watchman cried, and told the king. And the king said, If he be alone, there is tidings in his mouth. And he came apace, and drew near. . . .

And the king said, Is the young man Absalom safe? . . .

And the king said unto Cushi, Is the young man Absalom safe? And Cushi answered, The enemies of my lord the king, and all that rise against thee to do thee hurt, be as that young man is. And the king was much moved, and went up to the chamber over the gate, and wept: and as he went, thus he said, O my son Absalom, my son, my son Absalom! would God I had died for thee, O Absalom, my son, my son!

When a Father's Heart Breaks
The Story of David and Absalom

The two books of Samuel are candid in their retelling of King David's life.

Although we know little of his early years at home with Jesse and his brothers, we do know that he was a shepherd and songwriter who felt God's hand upon him when he confronted the giant Goliath. When he meets Jonathan, we are moved by the depth of their friendship and the grief of David's loss.

As king of Israel, we read how David dramatically transforms the tribes into a nation, while still battling his own dark desires and lust. Scripture describes unflinchingly David's act of adultery with Bathsheba and his order that sent Bathsheba's husband Uriah, a soldier, to his death. Later we read of the disastrous family conflict that followed the rape of David's daughter Tamar by her brother Amnon, and the subsequent death of Amnon at the hands of his brother Absalom. Finally, we learn of the great conspiracy that turned Absalom against his father David, followed by more battles and then the death of Absalom.

As David awaited news of his son, his watchman scanned the horizon for a runner. When one appeared, a second ran many steps behind. This first runner congratulated the king on the great victory over Absalom. And then David asked, "What about the young man Absalom?" The runner hedged and would not give David the news.

The second runner also congratulated the king on the victory. Again, David asked about the young man

Absalom. The Cushite runner replied, "The enemies of my lord the king and all that rise against thee to do thee hurt be like that young man."

Finally the king received the news of the death of Absalom who had been executed with a javelin by David's own commander, Joab.

How many nights did the king roam the corridors of his palace unable to sleep? In how many nightmares did the king see his son Absalom, held fast by his long hair tangled in tree branches—and then run through by the weapon of his own army commander?

For many nights there were those in the palace who heard their king weeping.

And the king was much moved, and went up to the chamber over the gate, and wept: and as he went, thus he said, O my son Absalom, my son, my son Absalom! would God I had died for thee, O Absalom, my son, my son!
2 SAMUEL 18:33

Can you imagine his grief?

When a Father's Heart Breaks

Think It Over

There is nothing like the shock of a middle-of-the-night phone call and the voice at the other end that tells you your "Absalom" is in trouble, or has been badly hurt...or is dead. How can a man prepare himself for that?

When a son or daughter disappoints you and the "what did I do wrong" thoughts begin to haunt you, what does scripture teach? Read Proverbs 23:7; Lamentations 3:21–26; Philippians 4:19. Every parent makes mistakes, but every child is also an individual who is responsible for the decisions he or she makes.

Read the following verse. How do you measure up to these words?

And, ye fathers, provoke not your children to wrath:
but bring them up in the nurture and admonition of the Lord.
EPHESIANS 6:4

20. The Wisest Son in the World
Scripture from 2 Samuel 12, 1 Kings 1-3, and Proverbs 1

[Nathan the prophet confronts David about his sin with Bathsheba, the wife of Uriah.] And David said unto Nathan, I have sinned against the LORD. And Nathan said unto David, The LORD also hath put away thy sin; thou shalt not die. Howbeit, because by this deed thou hast given great occasion to the enemies of the LORD to blaspheme, the child also that is born unto thee shall surely die. And Nathan departed unto his house. And the LORD struck the child that Uriah's wife bare unto David, and it was very sick. . . .

And it came to pass on the seventh day, that the child died. . . .

And David comforted Bathsheba his wife, and went in unto her, and lay with her: and she bare a son, and he called his name Solomon: and the LORD loved him.

[David's son Adonijah sets himself up as king at the close of David's reign.]

Wherefore Nathan spake unto Bathsheba the mother of Solomon, saying, Hast thou not heard that Adonijah the son of Haggith doth reign, and David our lord knoweth it not? Now therefore come, let me, I pray thee, give thee counsel, that thou mayest save thine own life, and the life of thy son Solomon. Go and get thee in unto king David, and say unto him, Didst not thou, my lord, O king, swear unto thine handmaid, saying, Assuredly Solomon thy son shall reign after me, and he shall sit upon my throne? why then doth Adonijah reign? [Bathsheba did as Nathan suggested.]

And the king sware, and said, As the LORD liveth,

that hath redeemed my soul out of all distress, even as I sware unto thee by the LORD God of Israel, saying, Assuredly Solomon thy son shall reign after me, and he shall sit upon my throne in my stead; even so will I certainly do this day. . . .

So Zadok the priest, and Nathan the prophet, and Benaiah the son of Jehoiada, and the Cherethites, and the Pelethites, went down, and caused Solomon to ride upon king David's mule, and brought him to Gihon. And Zadok the priest took an horn of oil out of the tabernacle, and anointed Solomon. And they blew the trumpet; and all the people said, God save king Solomon.

And all the people came up after him, and the people piped with pipes, and rejoiced with great joy, so that the earth rent with the sound of them. . . .

Now the days of David drew nigh that he should die; and he charged Solomon his son, saying, I go the way of all the earth: be thou strong therefore, and shew thyself a man; and keep the charge of the LORD thy God, to walk in his ways, to keep his statutes, and his commandments, and his judgments, and his testimonies, as it is written in the law of Moses, that thou mayest prosper in all that thou doest, and whithersoever thou turnest thyself: That the LORD may continue his word which he spake concerning me, saying, If thy children take heed to their way, to walk before me in truth with all their heart and with all their soul, there shall not fail thee (said he) a man on the throne of Israel.

[When Solomon was king he asked the Lord for wisdom.]

Give therefore thy servant an understanding heart to judge thy people, that I may discern between good and bad: for who is able to judge this thy so great a people?

The Wisest Son in the World
The Story of David and Solomon

What do we know about Solomon, the wisest man in his world?

1. His mother was Bathsheba. He was not the infant conceived when David committed adultery—that child died seven days after birth. But God graciously allowed Bathsheba to quickly conceive again, and this time she gave birth to Solomon.

2. Solomon was not the next in line to David's throne. He became king after a series of intrigues and the defeat of his brothers Absalom and Adonijah.

3. Solomon seems to have inherited his father's eye for beautiful women. While considered the wisest in all the land, he also had the reputation of being a womanizer. Many of his seven hundred marriages were for political reasons.

4. Like his father, Solomon was a wordsmith, or at least the collector of wise sayings and proverbs. Many concern the father-son relationship.

Early in King Solomon's reign, when God asked what gift he would want, Solomon requested wisdom. An observer of his father's follies and at times poor judgment, Solomon craved discernment. But where his father possessed the common touch, which won him legions of supporters, Solomon seemed to desire a more sophisticated life. No sheepfolds or rural rubes for him. His was a world of magnificent architecture (he built God's glorious temple in Jerusalem), rich fabrics and jewels befitting the Queen of Sheba, and a penchant for world travel and associating with peoples of other cultures.

Sadly, Solomon's search for wisdom and the finer things of life also led him into the acceptance, if not dedication, to other gods and ways of worshiping those gods. If only he had possessed David's singular love of God! Solomon's flirting with heathen religions and the establishment of the same in his homeland caused God, upon the king's death, to divide the kingdom into two separate entities.

Hundreds of years later, Jesus said these wise words, which could have described the fate of Israel after Solomon's reign:

> *Every kingdom divided against itself is brought*
> *to desolation; and every city or house divided*
> *against itself shall not stand.*
> MATTHEW 12:25

Did David and Solomon ever have a heart-to-heart over what is truth, and that the greatest of all wisdom is to love the Lord your God with all your heart, soul, and mind? Did the wisest man in all the world understand the need to be solely devoted to one God?

The Wisest Son in the World

Think It Over

One of Solomon's wise sayings, found in Proverbs 3:5–6, has become the life slogan for parents through the ages: "Trust in the LORD with all thine heart; and lean not unto thine own understanding. In all thy ways acknowledge him, and he shall direct thy paths." How can a father further impress this truth upon his children?

Here is another of Solomon's proverbs to make your own: "As a north wind brings rain, so a sly tongue brings angry looks" (Proverbs 25:23 NIV). What excellent advice for fathers! Sarcasm is not appropriate for children, so what kind of "language" should you use with your kids?

Finally, read Solomon's words for dads to pass on to their offspring: "Hearken unto thy father that begat thee, and despise not thy mother when she is old. Buy the truth, and sell it not; also wisdom, and instruction, and understanding" (Proverbs 23:22–23). How can you help your kids "buy the truth"?

The fear of the LORD
is the beginning of knowledge:
but fools despise wisdom and instruction.
PROVERBS 1:7

21. When Mother Is Away from God
Scripture from Hosea 1, 3

The word of the LORD that came unto Hosea, the son of Beeri. . . . And the LORD said to Hosea, Go, take unto thee a wife of whoredoms and children of whoredoms: for the land hath committed great whoredom, departing from the LORD.

So he went and took Gomer the daughter of Diblaim; which conceived, and bare him a son. And the LORD said unto him, Call his name Jezreel; for. . .I will break the bow of Israel, in the valley of Jezreel.

And she conceived again, and bare a daughter. And God said unto him, Call her name Loruhamah: for I will no more have mercy upon the house of Israel; but I will utterly take them away. . . .

Now when she had weaned Loruhamah, she conceived, and bare a son. Then said God, Call his name Loammi: for ye are not my people, and I will not be your God. [Despite Gomer's sinful behavior, God tells Hosea to return to his wife.]

Then said the LORD unto me, Go yet, love a woman beloved of her friend, yet an adulteress, according to the love of the LORD toward the children of Israel, who look to other gods, and love flagons of wine. So I bought her to me for fifteen pieces of silver, and for an homer of barley, and an half homer of barley: And I said unto her, Thou shalt abide for me many days; thou shalt not play the harlot, and thou shalt not be for another man: so will I also be for thee.

When Mother Is Away from God
The Story of Hosea and His Children

According to a much-read blog on the Internet, recently a pastor stood in his pulpit and attempted to make excuses for his wife's changes in behavior; that is, her absence from church and disinterest in the church family.

Overwhelmed by the situation, the pastor could only stand and repeat over and over, "I'm sorry. . .I'm sorry." He could not find the words to tell his congregation what was happening in his life. Finally, he put his head on the pulpit and wept. "She's left me," he said simply. "My wife has left me and our kids for another kind of life." A few persons in the congregation that morning were not shocked. Behind their bulletins they sniffed, "Well, what would you expect from that kind of woman?"

My heart goes out to any father who must tell the children that his wife, their mother, has not been faithful and has left the home.

On first reading Hosea's story of his relationship with his wife Gomer, one would think this pastor's dilemma is a carbon copy of Hosea's situation. They do have much in common, but they are not the same.

The cause of Hosea's heartbreak was a "God thing." God directed Hosea to marry Gomer, a prostitute, to illustrate the pain He felt at the wayward nature of His people, Israel. Through the ups and downs of Hosea and Gomer's relationship, we can see in painful detail God's unswerving love for His people and His magnificent power of forgiveness.

We can imagine Hosea's pain on the day he was

forced to tell the children about their mother's departure. Like any dad, he probably blamed himself. ("Been too busy being a prophet.") However, unlike the pastor in the blog, Hosea was determined to find Gomer and bring her home. Reading the text closely, you understand that such a strong instinct came from God. In our language, He commanded Hosea to "Find her . . . seek her out. . .demonstrate your love for her."

And so Hosea did. While the biblical details are sketchy, Hosea appears to go back to the bad part of town, where he found Gomer in the first place—a spot where human lives are up for bidding, where evil consumers buy love with no thoughts of love.

When Hosea finds his beloved Gomer, he obeys his heart and God's direction. He throws discretion to the wind and buys her back at so great a price.

Any father in this tragic situation must have answers for his children. If he and his wife reconcile, perhaps the best words to say would be what Hosea must have told Gomer as he took her home to her family: "Why did I follow after you, and buy you back? Because I love you."

Lord, why did You seek me out and buy me at so great a cost? "Because I love you" (see John 3:16).

When Mother Is Away from God

Think It Over

Hosea was an unusual father. Probably nothing like you, except in one major way—he loved his family. His story is in the Bible to teach the children of Israel that they are special in God's eyes.

To believers, Hosea and Gomer's story reminds us that while we are often rebellious and live selfish lives, we too were bought with a great price. Spend some time mulling over 1 Corinthians 7:23. Teach this to your children.

How does a father teach his children to respect their mother, even when she is away from God? How does Exodus 20:12 enter into this equation?

Granted, Hosea was a prophet, and it seems reasonable to believe that he had a special line of communication with God. But have you had a conversation with God lately? How do you know when God is giving instruction?

Is there a cost to discipleship? If so, what are you paying?

For the unbelieving husband is sanctified by the wife,
and the unbelieving wife is sanctified by the husband.
1 CORINTHIANS 7:14

22. And He Did Evil
Scripture from 2 Kings 18, 21

Now it came to pass in the third year of Hoshea son of Elah king of Israel, that Hezekiah the son of Ahaz king of Judah began to reign. . . .

And he did that which was right in the sight of the LORD, according to all that David his father did. He removed the high places, and brake the images, and cut down the groves, and brake in pieces the brasen serpent that Moses had made. . . .

And the LORD was with him; and he prospered whithersoever he went forth. . . .

[Following battles with the Assyrians, a devastating illness from which he recovered, and the birth of his son Manasseh, Hezekiah died.]

Manasseh was twelve years old when he began to reign, and reigned fifty and five years in Jerusalem. And his mother's name was Hephzibah.

And he did that which was evil in the sight of the LORD, after the abominations of the heathen, whom the LORD cast out before the children of Israel. For he built up again the high places which Hezekiah his father had destroyed; and he reared up altars for Baal, and made a grove, as did Ahab king of Israel; and worshipped all the host of heaven, and served them. And he built altars in the house of the LORD, of which the LORD said, In Jerusalem will I put my name. . . .

Moreover Manasseh shed innocent blood very much, till he had filled Jerusalem from one end to another; beside his sin wherewith he made Judah to sin, in doing that which was evil in the sight of the LORD.

And He Did Evil
The Story of Hezekiah and Manasseh

If you were an Old Testament king, can you imagine the thrill to be compared favorably to the greatest king of all—David? That would be like including an American president in the company of George Washington or Abraham Lincoln.

But that is what the Bible says: The Lord God obviously approved of King Hezekiah!

If, as psychologists have suggested, it is easier for a son or daughter to live with the "sins of the father" than with his accomplishments, that just might be the preface to this story. Such might have been the case of King Hezekiah's son and heir to the throne, Manasseh.

Indeed, there were very few bad marks against Hezekiah's twenty-nine-year reign on the throne. For Manasseh, dinner at home probably included his dad's detailed accounts of ripping out a town's heathen altars or the latest in Sennacherib's constant threats against Jerusalem—all to be taken seriously, but not by Manasseh.

There must have been times when Hephzibah, Manasseh's patient mother, complained to her husband that such dinner conversations were not very uplifting. And Hezekiah might have responded, "I'm not going to be around here forever, Hephzibah. One of these days that son of ours is going to be sitting on the throne of Judah, and then what?"

The "then what" happened much sooner than anyone expected—father Hezekiah died when Manasseh was a young boy. We don't know what transpired when the twelve–year-old was crowned king, whether influences within the court or politicos outside convinced the young king to reinstate the heathen religious practices that his father had abolished.

One would like to think that there were allies of his father still in court. There must have been cohorts of the old king who remembered those days when Hezekiah was near death and prayed, "I beseech thee, O LORD, remember now how I have walked before thee in truth and with a perfect heart, and have done that which is good in thy sight" (2 Kings 20:3)—and then wept bitterly. And who in Hezekiah's court could forget how the Lord had assured the prophet Isaiah that He would heal the king and add fifteen years to his life? When King Hezekiah regained his health, Jerusalem was spared from the hands of the Assyrians.

Did Manasseh hear these stories of God's goodness and faithfulness? Or was his father so wrapped up in the day-to-day business of being king that he never shared the faithfulness of the Lord God with his son?

Whatever the cause, a kingly father, who was compared to David, had a son whom the Lord called evil, and whose reign, to this very day, is looked upon as among the worst in Judah's history.

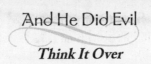

And He Did Evil

Think It Over

Why didn't God intervene and perform a miracle to straighten out King Manasseh? Are there times when the Lord lets us make our bed and then lie in it? If your life were to be printed in book form, which part would you like left out?

Reading Hezekiah's prayer on his supposed deathbed in chapter two, we realize there is no shame in crying or throwing ourselves upon God's mercy. Hezekiah's ancestor, King David, certainly did that. Have we as men become so strong and masculine that crying before the Lord is outside our experience? Have you felt like that?

Read and pray over Isaiah 49:25: "For I will contend with him that contendeth with thee, and I will save thy children." All in favor say aye?

You've been asked to think this over before, but it bears repeating: Successful dad, are you a success with your family?

> *Let nothing be done through strife or vainglory;*
> *but in lowliness of mind let each esteem*
> *other better than themselves.*
> PHILIPPIANS 2:3

23. My Wife Is Going to Have a What?!

Scripture from Luke 1

There was in the days of Herod, the king of Judaea, a certain priest named Zacharias, of the course of Abia: and his wife was of the daughters of Aaron, and her name was Elisabeth. And they were both righteous before God, walking in all the commandments and ordinances of the Lord blameless.

And they had no child, because that Elisabeth was barren, and they both were now well stricken in years.

And it came to pass, that while he executed the priest's office before God in the order of his course, according to the custom of the priest's office, his lot was to burn incense when he went into the temple of the Lord. . . .And there appeared unto him an angel of the Lord standing on the right side of the altar of incense.

And when Zacharias saw him, he was troubled, and fear fell upon him.

But the angel said unto him, Fear not, Zacharias: for thy prayer is heard; and thy wife Elisabeth shall bear thee a son, and thou shalt call his name John. And thou shalt have joy and gladness; and many shall rejoice at his birth. For he shall be great in the sight of the Lord, and shall drink neither wine nor strong drink; and he shall be filled with the Holy Ghost, even from his mother's womb. . . .

And Zacharias said unto the angel, Whereby shall I know this? for I am an old man, and my wife well stricken in years.

And the angel answering said unto him, I am Gabriel, that stand in the presence of God; and am sent to speak unto thee, and to shew thee these glad tidings. And, behold, thou shalt be dumb, and not able to speak, until the day that these things shall be performed, because thou believest not my words, which shall be fulfilled in their season. . . .

Now Elisabeth's full time came that she should be delivered; and she brought forth a son. And her neighbours and her cousins heard how the Lord had shewed great mercy upon her; and they rejoiced with her.

And it came to pass, that on the eighth day they came to circumcise the child; and they called him Zacharias, after the name of his father. And his mother answered and said, Not so; but he shall be called John. . . . And they made signs to his father, how he would have him called. And he asked for a writing table, and wrote, saying, His name is John. And they marvelled all.

And his mouth was opened immediately, and his tongue loosed, and he spake, and praised God. . . . And his father Zacharias was filled with the Holy Ghost, and prophesied, saying. . .And thou, child, shalt be called the prophet of the Highest: for thou shalt go before the face of the Lord to prepare his ways; to give knowledge of salvation unto his people by the remission of their sins, through the tender mercy of our God; whereby the dayspring from on high hath visited us, to give light to them that sit in darkness and in the shadow of death, to guide our feet into the way of peace.

And the child grew, and waxed strong in spirit, and was in the deserts till the day of his shewing unto Israel.

My Wife Is Going to Have a What?!
The Story of Zacharias and John

What possible relevance does this story have for me today, you ask. The answer is a heartfelt "Plenty!" In all probability, you're reading the devotionals in this book because you are already a father. You have discovered the sheer bliss of "daddyhood," and your wife has become well acquainted with the bone-numbing tiredness of being a mom.

Like you, Zacharias undoubtedly experienced the joys of being a dad. But unlike most of you, he had a long time to prepare for fatherhood. And what he brings to the "job," his qualifications for fatherhood, are part of what makes this story so relevant for all dads.

Zacharias's Gifts for Fatherhood
(According to Luke 1)

- He was righteous before God (verse 6). Zacharias was upright in God's sight. He could be trusted. He kept the Lord's ordinances and rules. When he messed up, he asked for forgiveness. He was fair in his dealings with others.
Into this family, God wanted His Son's forerunner to be born.
- He was a pray-er (verse 13). Zacharias occupied a position of responsibility in the temple and community. Besides his lineage from the tribe of Levi, he was entrusted with responsibility because he depended upon the Lord for wisdom and strength. His wife, too, strengthened his prayer life.

Into this family, God entrusted the child born to be His Son's evangelist.

- He had a joyful and happy disposition (verse 14). Is it too farfetched to believe Zacharias had a sense of humor? His wife Elisabeth certainly had one. An angel promised him joy and gladness. It sounds as if this would be a home where happiness would dwell.

Into this family, God gave a child with attributes to be His Son's coworker.

- He was patient (entire chapter). Throughout his silence, Zacharias was patient. Impatience is a negative force that can make a home a miserable place. Zacharias learned from experience that patience and peace are necessary.

Into this family, God entrusted a child to point the lost to His Son.

- He found the power to praise God (verse 64). After nine months of silence, old Zacharias still had praise in his heart. That's what a baby can do. But there was something more than that in his words of praise. Zacharias was recognizing God's faithfulness.

Into this family, God allowed John to be born, the one who would prepare the way for God's Son Jesus.

The Lord's hand was with him (verse 66). How appropriate this is for a new dad! How many times does a dad reach down into a crib to feel little fingers wrap around his finger? When the child is older, it's a thrill to feel a hand reach for yours as you cross a street. When you know that God's hand is close and available, you are filled with a sense of purpose and peace.

My Wife Is Going to Have a What?!

Think It Over

Think about your child's good friends. What do you know about their parents? If the kids are staying in your home for overnights and the like, make it a point to get acquainted with them. With your child's permission, invite them to go to church with you sometime. You might meet a modern-day version of Zacharias and Elisabeth, a couple who could bless you as much as your friendship blesses them.

Zacharias's praise to God (Luke 1:67–79) is an outstanding bit of verse. Verse 76 reads that John would be a "prophet of the Highest." How did John prepare the way for Jesus? (Read Luke 3:1–18.)

Reflect on the excitement and joy you experienced with your first child. In all probability it brought you closer to your wife. In what way did that event bring you closer to God?

Compare Luke 1:80 to Luke 2:52.

> *Like as a father pitieth his children,*
> *so the LORD pitieth them that fear him.*
> PSALM 103:13

24. When There's a Stepchild
Scripture from Matthew 1 and Luke 2

The book of the generation of Jesus Christ, the son of David, the son of Abraham. . . .

[Then follows forty-two generations from Abraham to Jesus Christ.]

And Jacob begat Joseph the husband of Mary, of whom was born Jesus, who is called Christ. . . .

Now the birth of Jesus Christ was on this wise: When as his mother Mary was espoused to Joseph, before they came together, she was found with child of the Holy Ghost. Then Joseph her husband, being a just man, and not willing to make her a public example, was minded to put her away privily. But while he thought on these things, behold, the angel of the LORD appeared unto him in a dream, saying, Joseph, thou son of David, fear not to take unto thee Mary thy wife: for that which is conceived in her is of the Holy Ghost.

And she shall bring forth a son, and thou shalt call his name JESUS: for he shall save his people from their sins.

Now all this was done, that it might be fulfilled which was spoken of the Lord by the prophet, saying, Behold, a virgin shall be with child, and shall bring forth a son, and they shall call his name Emmanuel, which being interpreted is, God with us.

Then Joseph being raised from sleep did as the angel of the Lord had bidden him, and took unto him his wife: And knew her not till she had brought forth her firstborn son: and he called his name JESUS.

And it came to pass in those days, that there went out a decree from Caesar Augustus that all the world should be taxed. . . . And all went to be taxed, every one into his own city.

And Joseph also went up from Galilee, out of the city of Nazareth, into Judaea, unto the city of David, which is called Bethlehem; (because he was of the house and lineage of David). . . . And so it was, that, while they were there, the days were accomplished that she should be delivered.

And she brought forth her firstborn son, and wrapped him in swaddling clothes, and laid him in a manger; because there was no room for them in the inn. . . .

And when he was twelve years old, they went up to Jerusalem after the custom of the feast. And when they had fulfilled the days, as they returned, the child Jesus tarried behind in Jerusalem; and Joseph and his mother knew not of it.

But they, supposing him to have been in the company, went a day's journey; and they sought him among their kinsfolk and acquaintance. And when they found him not, they turned back again to Jerusalem, seeking him.

And it came to pass, that after three days they found him in the temple, sitting in the midst of the doctors, both hearing them, and asking them questions. And all that heard him were astonished at his understanding and answers.

And when they saw him, they were amazed: and his mother said unto him, Son, why hast thou thus dealt with us? behold, thy father and I have sought thee sorrowing. And he said unto them, How is it that ye sought me? wist ye not that I must be about my Father's business?

And they understood not the saying which he spake unto them.

And he went down with them, and came to Nazareth, and was subject unto them: but his mother kept all these sayings in her heart. And Jesus increased in wisdom and stature, and in favour with God and man.

When There's a Stepchild
The Story of Joseph and Jesus

Nothing could be more heart-sickening than to believe that your beloved has been unfaithful to you—and that she's pregnant with someone else's baby!

That's how it was with Joseph and his fiancée Mary. Joseph was a simple man, a carpenter by trade. Mary might have been the only girl he ever loved. Coming from a small town as he did, the boys set their eyes on a girl at a young age, which started in motion a process involving her parents and the young man's folks.

If the citizens of Nazareth were like those of any small town, it isn't a stretch of the imagination to believe that everyone knew everybody else's business. When tongues wagged about Mary and her pregnant look, Joseph undoubtedly picked up on it. Devastated, Joseph went so far as to consider calling off their engagement, according to the gospel account.

Then the most miraculous thing happened. While he was sleeping, an angel of the Lord suddenly appeared to him in a dream. The angel said, "Joseph, thou son of David, fear not to take unto thee Mary thy wife: for that which is conceived in her is of the Holy Ghost. And she shall bring forth a son, and thou shalt call his name JESUS: for he shall save his people from their sins" (Matthew 1:20–21).

Joseph accepted the angel's pronouncement, and he and Mary were married. Soon after that, they took that fateful trip to Bethlehem for the registration. If Joseph were writing about this today, he might report that the birth of Mary's child in Bethlehem was the proudest day of his life. He had a son!

But how was Joseph to think of his parental relationship to Jesus? The angel had told him about the Holy Spirit's involvement in Jesus' conception. Nevertheless, Joseph carried out his role as father, working long hours in his shop to provide for Mary and Jesus, and, as any Middle Eastern father, we imagine having a hand in Jesus' discipline and instruction. He surely modeled manhood for his boy.

When Mary and Joseph took Jesus to the temple for the rites of childhood, Joseph was part of the rituals. And when they thought He was lost, Joseph undoubtedly felt the same pangs in his chest that any father would have.

Together, Mary and Joseph had four more sons: Joseph Jr., Simon, Jude, and James. One can only speculate what life was like in their Nazareth home—how Jesus related to His siblings, what they knew of His mission.

In time, Joseph disappears from the gospel narrative. Scholars presume he died before Jesus was sent to the cross since Mary is described in scripture as being alone at Calvary (and later she alone was delivered into the disciple John's care).

As a man of faith who trusted God to lead him, and as a stepfather who did not shirk from his responsibilities, Joseph of Nazareth is a man to be praised.

When There's a Stepchild

Think It Over

Joseph's story may be too unique to hold out as a model for dads, but what does he have to say to fathers of stepchildren or adopted or foster kids?

How do you think Joseph felt when the twelve-year-old Jesus said, "I must be about my Father's business"? How have you reacted when a son or daughter has said to you, "You just don't understand me"?

The New Testament gives no clues that Jesus ever thought about His growing-up years in Joseph's home. But His enemies tried to make Him like everyone else by accusing Him of being only a carpenter's son. Jesus didn't need to "learn" anything about ministry, but what qualities of an effective pastor might Jesus have picked up in Joseph's shop? How can you apply these to your relationship with your children?

Do you treat your kids differently? Is protection more of a mother thing?

And all thy children shall be taught of the Lord;
and great shall be the peace of thy children.
ISAIAH 54:13

25. A Fishy Family Business

Scripture from Matthew 4, 27 and Mark 1

And Jesus, walking by the sea of Galilee, saw two brethren, Simon called Peter, and Andrew his brother, casting a net into the sea: for they were fishers.

And he saith unto them, Follow me, and I will make you fishers of men. And they straightway left their nets, and followed him.

And going on from thence, he saw other two brethren, James the son of Zebedee, and John his brother, in a ship with Zebedee their father, mending their nets; and he called them. And they immediately left the ship and their father, and followed him. . . .

And many women were there [at the crucifixion] beholding afar off, which followed Jesus from Galilee, ministering unto him: Among which was Mary Magdalene, and Mary the mother of James and Joses, and the mother of Zebedee's children. . . .

Now as he walked by the sea of Galilee, he saw Simon and Andrew his brother casting a net into the sea: for they were fishers. And Jesus said unto them, Come ye after me, and I will make you to become fishers of men.

And straightway they forsook their nets, and followed him.

And when he had gone a little farther thence, he saw James the son of Zebedee, and John his brother, who also were in the ship mending their nets. And straightway he called them: and they left their father Zebedee in the ship with the hired servants, and went after him.

A Fishy Family Business
The Story of Zebedee and James and John

To me, the story of Zebedee is much more than a few verses in the Bible.

You see, my father was a Zebedee. His name was Arthur, but everyone called him Art. He fished a lot but never for a living. Dad was a sign painter. He was proud of his work, and he had every reason to be. Unlike Zebedee, during his working years, Dad always labored for someone else. He never had the finances or self-assurance to launch out on his own.

Evidently, Zebedee had his two sons James and John working for him—the two, by the way, known as the "sons of thunder." Peter and Andrew appear to have been part of Zebedee's fishing crew, too. Yes, for a while he had a couple of boatloads of hardworking, skilled fishermen. . .and then Jesus came into the picture.

When Jesus met them at the Sea of Galilee, Zebedee lost his workforce. Jesus' invitation to Zebedee's four fishermen was immediately accepted. They weren't going to be catching fish anymore. They were going to be fishers of men.

At one point in his life, my dad decided he'd take a leap of faith and open his own sign shop. His proviso was that I'd join him in the business. To a high school kid, that eventuality seemed so far off it was easy to agree to join him.

Almost immediately, Dad had business cards printed with both our names. Our company name was ArtSon. Dad never quit his day job, but he was busy planning and dreaming for the success of ArtSon. . .and then Jesus came into the picture.

I received a call to ministry at a church youth camp in the Santa Cruz (California) Mountains. Unlike James and John, it took a week of prayer and counseling to say "yes" to God.

Not one to hold in good news, the minute I got home from camp, I made the big announcement. "I'm going to be a minister, probably a pastor, for the church!" I saw my dad's face sag, and then I remembered.

Dad never dropped his paintbrush to follow Jesus Christ. And, as far as we know, Zebedee didn't get rid of his nets either. But to Zebedee's everlasting credit, he did not keep his sons from fulfilling their calling. Neither did my dad.

My dad never kept my mother from committing her life to Christ and participating in all that that life had to offer. It's a thrill to realize that Zebedee's wife, "the mother of Zebedee's sons" was at the cross with the other women, including Mary, Jesus' mother.

The Greek form of the name Zebedee means "gift." In many ways, he lived up to his name. His gift to the Christian world was the release of his sons and his wife to Jesus and ministry.

I can't help but wish my dad had given that gift to himself.

A Fishy Family Business

Think It Over

Is God still calling men and women into His service? Has He ever spoken to you about ministry? Would you be willing to respond positively to His call? Read and respond to Colossians 1:9.

There was a time when children automatically entered the family business. Is today's independence a gift from God? How does the Lord use our independence for His good?

When your child was dedicated or baptized, you accepted a responsibility in training him or her in the ways of the Spirit. How have you done?

Paraphrase Romans 12:6–8 (NIV) to match your kids' gifts: "We have different gifts, according to the grace given us. If a man's gift is prophesying, let him use it in proportion to his faith. If it is serving, let him serve; if it is teaching, let him teach; if it is encouraging, let him encourage; if it is contributing to the needs of others, let him give generously; if it is leadership, let him govern diligently; if it is showing mercy, let him do it cheerfully."

For God's gifts and his call are irrevocable.
ROMANS 11:29 NIV

26. A Father's Love

And [Jesus] said, A certain man had two sons: And the younger of them said to his father, Father, give me the portion of goods that falleth to me. And he divided unto them his living.

And not many days after the younger son gathered all together, and took his journey into a far country, and there wasted his substance with riotous living. And when he had spent all, there arose a mighty famine in that land; and he began to be in want.

And he went and joined himself to a citizen of that country; and he sent him into his fields to feed swine. And he would fain have filled his belly with the husks that the swine did eat: and no man gave unto him.

And when he came to himself, he said, How many hired servants of my father's have bread enough and to spare, and I perish with hunger! I will arise and go to my father, and will say unto him, Father, I have sinned against heaven, and before thee, and am no more worthy to be called thy son: make me as one of thy hired servants.

And he arose, and came to his father. But when he was yet a great way off, his father saw him, and had compassion, and ran, and fell on his neck, and kissed him. . . .

The father said to his servants, Bring forth the best robe, and put it on him; and put a ring on his hand, and shoes on his feet: And bring hither the fatted calf, and kill it; and let us eat, and be merry: For this my son was dead, and is alive again; he was lost, and is found. And they began to be merry.

A Father's Love
The Story of a Father and His Younger Son

Jesus often grabbed His listeners' minds and hearts with powerful stories that were also teaching tools.

- Audience: Unidentified crowd, including tax collectors and "sinners," Pharisees, and teachers of the law.
- Location: Probably in the Jerusalem area.
- Complaints: The Pharisees and teachers of the law are unhappy that Jesus is associating with the likes of sinful people, including the much despised tax collectors.
- The teaching: Jesus tells three stories in Luke 15: the lost coin, the lost son, and the lost sheep. We don't know which story the audience liked best, but it's a safe guess that the story of the lost, or prodigal, son, created the most interest. After all, the wayward son's demands and how the father gives in to them were certainly not typical of first-century parenting. But the underlying point is something they don't expect.

Jesus' story leaves many details to our imagination. What parent would even listen to a demanding adolescent or an adult child with such an adolescent attitude?

Further, we don't know what provoked the younger son's demand for his share of the family estate. We do know that he blew his whole inheritance on what the

King James Version calls "riotous living." But who could foresee the famine, the empty pockets, the pig farmer's disgust, the disappointment, and the shame?

Jesus told His enthralled listeners, "Then the boy came to his senses." Saying those words, He must have looked squarely into the faces of fathers who had senseless children, or who were senseless themselves.

Jesus spends no time relating the mischief and sin to which the young son exposed himself. Instead, he focuses in on the boy's father, the father who often asked himself, Did I do the right thing? Where is he tonight? Is he safe from harm? God only knows how many times he went to the end of the road to see if his son might be on the horizon—coming home.

And finally, one day, according to Jesus' story, the father's heart quickened, for walking up the dusty road was his younger boy. Forgetting his age and what the neighbors might think, old dad runs and meets the boy halfway. And seemingly the first words out of the boy's mouth were, "Father, I have sinned."

The father's words of forgiveness are not recorded in the parable, but his kiss and hug were all the evidence needed.

The point of this parable? Father God, like earthly dads, loves us in spite of the many ways we disappoint Him. Like the father of the lost son, He will meet His son or daughter when we cry out to Him, embracing us with forgiveness.

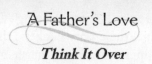

Think It Over

Like the other parables of Jesus, the parable of the lost son has one major point: Despite our sinful behavior, our Father God loves and forgives us.

Think about the father in the parable. What emotions has he experienced? Ephesians 4:32 describes human forgiveness. "Kindliness" and "compassion" are the operative traits here. They should be ingrained in a father's spirit when forgiving a child.

We have no idea if the father in Jesus' parable had a wife backing him or ridiculing him as he gave the younger son his share of the requested estate. We do know that it was the father who watched and waited, and then met his son on the road to home. Consider the differences between a dad's and a mom's love toward the kids—or is there a difference?

What about the converse of this situation—how does a father ask forgiveness for a wrong he has done to a daughter or son? Read Hebrews 4:16 and apply its truth to this situation.

What do you think the father's gifts to the boy represent? Consider the robe, the ring, the shoes, and the feast.

And above all things have fervent charity among yourselves:
for charity shall cover the multitude of sins.
Use hospitality one to another without grudging.
1 PETER 4:8–9

27. A Father's Disappointment
Scripture from Luke 15 and Proverbs 4

And he [Jesus] said, A certain man had two sons. . . . Now his elder son was in the field: and as he came and drew nigh to the house, he heard musick and dancing. And he called one of the servants, and asked what these things meant.

And he said unto him, Thy brother is come; and thy father hath killed the fatted calf, because he hath received him safe and sound.

And he was angry, and would not go in: therefore came his father out, and intreated him. And he answering said to his father, Lo, these many years do I serve thee, neither transgressed I at any time thy commandment: and yet thou never gavest me a kid, that I might make merry with my friends:

But as soon as this thy son was come, which hath devoured thy living with harlots, thou hast killed for him the fatted calf.

And he said unto him, Son, thou art ever with me, and all that I have is thine. It was meet that we should make merry, and be glad: for this thy brother was dead, and is alive again; and was lost, and is found.

Hear, ye children, the instruction of a father, and attend to know understanding. For I give you good doctrine, forsake ye not my law.

For I was my father's son, tender and only beloved in the sight of my mother. He taught me also, and said unto me, Let thine heart retain my words: keep my commandments, and live.

Get wisdom, get understanding: forget it not; neither decline from the words of my mouth. Forsake her not, and she shall preserve thee: love her, and she shall keep thee.

Wisdom is the principal thing; therefore get wisdom: and with all thy getting get understanding. Exalt her, and she shall promote thee: she shall bring thee to honour, when thou dost embrace her.

She shall give to thine head an ornament of grace: a crown of glory shall she deliver to thee.

A Father's Disappointment
The Story of a Father and His Older Son

Jesus' story of the lost son continues, but now the focus shifts to the older son, the one who stayed at home. Again, we let our imaginations take over as we probe behind the scenes.

At the father's ranch house there are lights in every window and the sound of music pours out the open doors. There is a plump calf in the cooking pit, and farmhands carry in baskets of fresh fruit and veggies. In the kitchen, a baker forms fancy date cakes, while a steward pours cups of well-aged beverages.

Moving among his guests is the father with the younger son on his arm. Neighbors whisper to each other how fine the boy looks. "You've grown up to be a handsome young man," one local comments.

Before the embarrassed boy can answer, his father explains that his son has been lost but is now at home. To mark the occasion, he is celebrating with this great party, and also presenting the boy with a newly tailored outfit and an heirloom signet ring.

"And what about your older son? I haven't seen . . ." one neighbor queries.

The father quickly looks around. "Why, he must be around here somewhere." Turning, he asks his younger son, "Have you seen your brother?"

"He's on the back porch. He won't come in."

The father pats his younger son on the arm. "You stay here. I'm going out to talk with him."

Sure enough, sitting on the back steps in the dark is the angry older son. When his father sits down beside him, the young man scoots away. "Come on, tell me what's bothering you."

After a long pause, the older son begins to open up. "Father, I've tried to be a faithful son for all these years. I've never disobeyed you and I've tried not to disappoint you. Right?"

"Except maybe now, son."

"And who gets rewarded? My sneaky brother! The no-good member of our family who conned you into giving him our inheritance and then ran away to the city."

"But son, you . . ."

"And that's not all. He squandered away our money doing who knows what!"

"Is there anything else you want to say?" A long pause follows. "Anything more?"

Quietly, the son adds, "Father, all these years I've worked like a slave for you, and you've never even given me a scrawny goat!" He moves farther away from his dad. "Why?"

With a sigh, his father tries to put his arm around his son's shoulders, but the older son shrugs it away. Inside the house, there is still dancing and music.

Finally he clears his throat and says, "My son, you are always with me. I have always been able to count on you. You know everything I have is yours." When he receives no response, he goes on. "Put yourself in my place. I believed your brother was dead—but he's not, he's alive! He's come home to us. The lost has been found."

Jesus told this story to the angry, self-centered Pharisees who did not understand a loving, forgiving God. It was Jesus' desire that they would see themselves as the older son. Perhaps the older son lives under your roof.

A Father's Disappointment
Think It Over

It can be frightening to see your own less-than-noble traits in your kids. Was the father taken by surprise by his older son's reaction? It wouldn't be surprising if he didn't find a quiet place somewhere and look closely at himself.

The older boy in Jesus' parable broke his father's heart as hurtfully as the younger. What was his sin? Can you relate it to 1 Corinthians 13:4–7?

Since Jesus was teaching this parable to an audience that included Pharisees and other self-righteous religious leaders, what was the part of the story He directed their way?

What could the father have done differently in handling his older son? Is there ever that kind of rivalry among your children? What do you do to intervene?

For God so loved the world,
that he gave his only begotten Son,
that whosoever believeth in him
should not perish, but have everlasting life.
JOHN 3:16

28. Trust and Obey
Scripture from John 4

When he was come into Galilee, the Galilaeans received him, having seen all the things that he did at Jerusalem at the feast: for they also went unto the feast.

So Jesus came again into Cana of Galilee, where he made the water wine. And there was a certain nobleman, whose son was sick at Capernaum. When he heard that Jesus was come out of Judaea into Galilee, he went unto him, and besought him that he would come down, and heal his son: for he was at the point of death.

Then said Jesus unto him, Except ye see signs and wonders, ye will not believe.

The nobleman saith unto him, Sir, come down ere my child die.

Jesus saith unto him, Go thy way; thy son liveth. And the man believed the word that Jesus had spoken unto him, and he went his way.

And as he was now going down, his servants met him, and told him, saying, Thy son liveth. Then enquired he of them the hour when he began to amend. And they said unto him, Yesterday at the seventh hour the fever left him.

So the father knew that it was at the same hour, in the which Jesus said unto him, Thy son liveth: and himself believed, and his whole house.

This is again the second miracle that Jesus did, when he was come out of Judaea into Galilee.

Trust and Obey
The Story of a Nobleman and His Son

Any dad who has ever stood at the bedside of a seriously ill child can relate to this event in Jesus' earthly ministry. As with many of Jesus' healings, no names are given to the cast of characters. There was no public relations firm writing news releases or notifying the public where Christ could be found, say between noon and two o'clock while in Capernaum, or in this case, Cana. This event is comparable to the healing of the centurion's servant (see Matthew 8:5–13).

John identifies Cana as the location of Jesus' first miracle—turning water into wine at a wedding feast—which is significant. Almost with a sense of sorrow, John acknowledges that the Galileans were welcoming not because Jesus was Messiah and could save them, but because of what He provided in amazing entertainment. Galilee was the Savior's home region; the crowds were "His people."

The royal official in this healing event was no doubt in service to Herod Antipas, son of King Herod the Great. He was stationed fifteen to twenty miles away in Capernaum, where his son lay ill.

The scripture tells us that the father was in Cana because he knew Jesus was going to be there. With a sick son at the center of his attention, he just may have canceled all appointments for the day and took off for Cana to have an encounter with Jesus.

At that Cana encounter, Jesus seems to speak to the father without compassion. The man has begged Him to come to Capernaum before his son dies. It appears that Jesus uses that moment to set the Galileans straight, telling them that it's the miracles that they believe in and not Him.

My heart goes out to the nobleman who was mustering all the faith he could when he said, "Sir, come down to Capernaum before my son dies." In those simple words, Jesus discovered a man of faith in that crowd, someone who wasn't just a curious thrill seeker. Jesus simply replied, "You may go. Your son will live."

Read carefully John 4:50: "And the man believed the word that Jesus had spoken unto him, and he went his way." Unlike the Galilean crowd, this father needed nothing more than Jesus' word that his son would live. There were no questions, no dialogue between an anxious parent and Jesus.

Father: Don't you want to see him? Maybe take his temp?
Jesus: Your son will live.
Father: But what about prescriptions?
Jesus: Your son will live.

And he lived! Even before the father arrived home, his servants met him with the good news. Moreover, they figured the healing took place at the exact moment Jesus said, "Your son will live." Praise God!

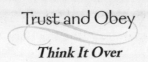

Think It Over

This encounter between Jesus and the nobleman should take your breath away! There's a gospel song with a chorus that went, "Such love, such wondrous love! . . . How wonderful is love like this!" Dad, do you believe it? Does your family know that "such love" has filled your heart and life? If not, tell them—or tell them again.

You've read it before, but read it again—Hebrews 11:1, or better yet, read the entire chapter, all forty verses. What do trust and faith have in common? How does obedience fit into the equation?

Now relate all this to the story of Jesus and the nobleman.

Finally, how do you and your family fit into this story?

Now faith is the substance of things hoped for,
the evidence of things not seen.
HEBREWS 11:1

And, behold, there cometh one of the rulers of the synagogue, Jairus by name; and when he saw him, he fell at his feet, and besought him greatly, saying, My little daughter lieth at the point of death: I pray thee, come and lay thy hands on her, that she may be healed; and she shall live.

And Jesus went with him; and much people followed him, and thronged him.

And a certain woman, which had an issue of blood twelve years, and had suffered many things of many physicians, and had spent all that she had, and was nothing bettered, but rather grew worse, when she had heard of Jesus, came in the press behind, and touched his garment.

For she said, If I may touch but his clothes, I shall be whole.

And straightway the fountain of her blood was dried up; and she felt in her body that she was healed of that plague.

And Jesus, immediately knowing in himself that virtue had gone out of him, turned him about in the press, and said, Who touched my clothes? And his disciples said unto him, Thou seest the multitude thronging thee, and sayest thou, Who touched me?

And he looked round about to see her that had done this thing.

But the woman fearing and trembling, knowing what was done in her, came and fell down before him, and told him all the truth.

And he said unto her, Daughter, thy faith hath made thee whole; go in peace, and be whole of thy plague.

While he yet spake, there came from the ruler of the synagogue's house certain which said, Thy daughter is dead: why troublest thou the Master any further?

As soon as Jesus heard the word that was spoken, he saith unto the ruler of the synagogue, Be not afraid, only believe. And he suffered no man to follow him, save Peter, and James, and John the brother of James.

And he cometh to the house of the ruler of the synagogue, and seeth the tumult, and them that wept and wailed greatly. And when he was come in, he saith unto them, Why make ye this ado, and weep? the damsel is not dead, but sleepeth.

And they laughed him to scorn. But when he had put them all out, he taketh the father and the mother of the damsel, and them that were with him, and entereth in where the damsel was lying.

And he took the damsel by the hand, and said unto her, *Talitha cumi*; which is, being interpreted, Damsel, I say unto thee, arise.

And straightway the damsel arose, and walked; for she was of the age of twelve years. And they were astonished with a great astonishment.

And he charged them straitly that no man should know it; and commanded that something should be given her to eat.

⌀

And many other signs truly did Jesus in the presence of his disciples, which are not written in this book: But these are written, that ye might believe that Jesus is the Christ, the Son of God; and that believing ye might have life through his name.

A Father and God's Timing
The Story of Jairus and His Daughter

There are few sights happier than seeing a family gathered together around their table, eating, laughing, and wiping away tears of joy. Such was the scene at Jairus's house minutes after Jesus left.

This meal was held at the recommendation of Jesus, after He brought Jairus's daughter back to life. Can you imagine the mealtime conversation?

"I said I was hungry, but I didn't say stuff me!" The twelve-year-old who had just passed from death back to life had quickly regained her independent spirit. Her father sat on one side, refilling his daughter's bowl with stew, while Mother refilled her cup with goat's milk.

"Papa, tell me again how you found Jesus and got Him to come here and see me."

"He was easy to find, honey," her father said, laughing. "It was getting to Him that was difficult."

Jairus's description of the crowd was not an unusual happening when the Healer came to town. It was the "signs and wonders" part of Jesus' ministry that seemed to excite the crowds. Of course that's why Jairus sought Him—his daughter on the verge of death. But getting to Him, and then getting Him to their house, was another matter.

"When I became rude and pushed people out of the way, I finally got to Him."

"Did He know who you were?"

"I don't know, honey. He doesn't seem to take much stock in that sort of thing."

As a leader of the synagogue, Jairus had prestige in

town. He could always go to the head of any line without a wait, and shopkeepers curried his patronage.

From Jesus' point of view, seeing a proud ruler of the synagogue on his knees in front of Him touched His heart. "Show me the way," was Jesus' response. "Let's all go!" responded the crowd.

"Then what took you so long?" the daughter asked.

"We'd not moved very far when Jesus stopped. 'Who touched me?' He asked the crowd." Jairus explained that a woman he'd seen around the synagogue, who had suffered years from a bleeding disorder, was the guilty party. "But all I could think about was you lying here at home."

"That's about the time we sent the servants out to find you," the girl's mother reported.

"They found me," Jairus said, his eyes filling with tears at the memory, "and gave me the news that our daughter was dead. You can imagine how a flash of resentment went through me. Here was this old woman taking up the time we needed for Jesus at our house."

"What did He say?"

"Jesus told the woman she was healed and told me not to be afraid, but to believe," was the father's reply. "I did believe!"

The daughter knew her father was a believer. He never believed in coincidence or luck. "It's God!" he'd say. So while the mourners grieved, and his wife covered the mirror, Jairus kept his fear at bay.

But when Jesus said, "Little girl, get up," Jairus shouted for joy!

Thus the hearty meal, the laughter, and the knowledge that the Lord's timing has nothing to do with clocks or our apprehension. All Jairus had to do was believe.

A Father and God's Timing

Think It Over

Panic sent Jairus out the door to find Jesus. Evidently this was his first resort. No doctors are mentioned in the narrative. Would such strong belief characterize you in a similar situation? In what ways does your family see your belief in God's mercies?

In Mark's gospel, the story of Jairus's daughter and the bleeding woman are not separated. Besides the fact that they happened simultaneously, what meaningful similarities or differences do you see between the two? What part does age play in the stories? Are there age issues in your family?

If you are like many fathers, you know how easy it is to run ahead of God. Yes, we do believe, but is our faith strong enough to let Him do it His way? We expect that of our kids—but can God expect that from us?

How do the following familiar verses of scripture relate to you?

> *Commit thy way unto the LORD. . . .*
> *Rest in the LORD, and wait patiently for him.*
> PSALM 37:5, 7

30. A Substitute Father
Scripture from 1 and 2 Timothy

Paul, an apostle of Jesus Christ by the commandment of God our Saviour, and Lord Jesus Christ, which is our hope; unto Timothy, my own son in the faith: Grace, mercy, and peace, from God our Father and Jesus Christ our Lord. . . .

But thou, O man of God, flee these things; and follow after righteousness, godliness, faith, love, patience, meekness. Fight the good fight of faith, lay hold on eternal life, whereunto thou art also called, and hast professed a good profession before many witnesses.

I thank God, whom I serve from my forefathers with pure conscience, that without ceasing I have remembrance of thee in my prayers night and day; greatly desiring to see thee, being mindful of thy tears, that I may be filled with joy;

When I call to remembrance the unfeigned faith that is in thee, which dwelt first in thy grandmother Lois, and thy mother Eunice; and I am persuaded that in thee also.

Wherefore I put thee in remembrance that thou stir up the gift of God, which is in thee by the putting on of my hands. For God hath not given us the spirit of fear; but of power, and of love, and of a sound mind. . . .

Hold fast the form of sound words, which thou hast heard of me, in faith and love which is in Christ Jesus. . . .

Thou therefore, my son, be strong in the grace that

is in Christ Jesus. And the things that thou hast heard of me among many witnesses, the same commit thou to faithful men, who shall be able to teach others also. Thou therefore endure hardness, as a good soldier of Jesus Christ. . . .

Consider what I say; and the Lord give thee understanding in all things. . . .

I charge thee therefore before God, and the Lord Jesus Christ, who shall judge the quick and the dead at his appearing and his kingdom; preach the word; be instant in season, out of season; reprove, rebuke, exhort with all long suffering and doctrine. . . .

But watch thou in all things, endure afflictions, do the work of an evangelist, make full proof of thy ministry.

For I am now ready to be offered, and the time of my departure is at hand. I have fought a good fight, I have finished my course, I have kept the faith: Henceforth there is laid up for me a crown of righteousness, which the Lord, the righteous judge, shall give me at that day: and not to me only, but unto all them also that love his appearing.

Do thy diligence to come shortly unto me: For Demas hath forsaken me, having loved this present world, and is departed unto Thessalonica; Crescens to Galatia, Titus unto Dalmatia. Only Luke is with me. Take Mark, and bring him with thee: for he is profitable to me for the ministry. . . .

The cloke that I left at Troas with Carpus, when thou comest, bring with thee, and the books, but especially the parchments. . . . Do thy diligence to come before winter. The Lord Jesus Christ be with thy spirit. Grace be with you. Amen.

A Substitute Father
The Story of Paul and Timothy

Paul is never mentioned in scripture as a father—but he surely thought of Timothy as his spiritual son. In fact, Timothy would become a strategic character in the formation of the first-century church.

There are several possibilities that may account for the silence about Timothy's biological father. The first is that he may have died soon after the boy was born in Lystra, which might explain the pivotal roles his grandmother and mother played in his spiritual development.

Another possibility is that Timothy's father had little if any influence on his son's life. Acts 16:1 tells us that Timothy's father was a Greek, while his mother was a Jewish Christian. It is further noted in Acts that before Paul would take the younger man on a missionary trip, he had to be circumcised so that his Greek parentage would not be a problem.

Worse than losing one's father physically is to have a parent who is present in the home but, for all intents and purposes, is absent. He's "too busy" to build a lasting father-son relationship. Maybe Timothy's father's Gentile faith was not what a Christian mother wanted for her son. There may have been major disagreements over the boy's education and religious training, which further separated Timothy from his dad. In order to keep the peace, Timothy's father may have emotionally removed himself from the situation.

When Paul came to Lystra, he found a young man whose mother and grandmother had provided him spiritual training from the Old Testament. In spite of an absentee father, Timothy had developed special abilities that could be built upon in missionary work. Reading Paul's letters to his "true son in the faith," we sense that he believed God had sent Timothy into his life for the growth of the Christian faith.

There is a poignant myth told in the Eastern church that goes like this. While the apostle Paul was imprisoned in Rome awaiting his last trial, Timothy's biological father was facing death in Lystra. With great passion, an imaginative storyteller repeats the father's last wish: "Timothy, I am destitute and poor, and I'm dying. Will you send me evidence of your success and wealth? Please remember, I am your father."

At the same moment, the apostle is writing to his "son in the faith," pastor of the church in Ephesus. Paraphrasing scripture, Paul says, "Do your best to come to me before winter, and bring my coat with you. Come quickly. I have fought the good fight. I have finished the race, I have kept the faith. The Lord be with your spirit."

Thank God for faithful fathers, and for those who are called to replace absentee dads.

A Substitute Father

Think It Over

What spiritual lessons did your father pass on to you? Was there someone in your life like Paul, who provided your spiritual education? How does that compare to what you are doing for your own kids?

Who in your home provides spiritual training to the family? Is there anyone else exerting Christian influence on your children? If there is, does that bother you or do you feel grateful? Would you rather assume more of that role with your kids?

How do you express loving support to your kids? Does that mean giving money, or have you found more personal ways to show your affection? Should this depend on the ages of your children?

Thou therefore, my son, be strong
in the grace that is in Christ Jesus.
2 TIMOTHY 2:1

[Jesus said these words to His disciples.]

And when thou prayest, thou shalt not be as the hypocrites are: for they love to pray standing in the synagogues and in the corners of the streets, that they may be seen of men. Verily I say unto you, They have their reward.

But thou, when thou prayest, enter into thy closet, and when thou hast shut thy door, pray to thy Father which is in secret; and thy Father which seeth in secret shall reward thee openly. But when ye pray, use not vain repetitions, as the heathen do: for they think that they shall be heard for their much speaking.

Be not ye therefore like unto them: for your Father knoweth what things ye have need of, before ye ask him.

And it came to pass, that, as he was praying in a certain place, when he ceased, one of his disciples said unto him, Lord, teach us to pray, as John also taught his disciples.

And he said unto them, When ye pray, say, Our Father which art in heaven, Hallowed be thy name. Thy kingdom come. Thy will be done, as in heaven, so in earth. Give us day by day our daily bread.

And forgive us our sins; for we also forgive every one that is indebted to us. And lead us not into temptation; but deliver us from evil.

And he said unto them, Which of you shall have a friend, and shall go unto him at midnight, and say unto him, Friend, lend me three loaves; for a friend of mine in his journey is come to me, and I have nothing to set before him?

And he from within shall answer and say, Trouble me not: the door is now shut, and my children are with me in bed; I cannot rise and give thee.

I say unto you, Though he will not rise and give him, because he is his friend, yet because of his importunity he will rise and give him as many as he needeth.

And I say unto you, Ask, and it shall be given you; seek, and ye shall find; knock, and it shall be opened unto you. For every one that asketh receiveth; and he that seeketh findeth; and to him that knocketh it shall be opened.

If a son shall ask bread of any of you that is a father, will he give him a stone? or if he ask a fish, will he for a fish give him a serpent? Or if he shall ask an egg, will he offer him a scorpion?

If ye then, being evil, know how to give good gifts unto your children: how much more shall your heavenly Father give the Holy Spirit to them that ask him?

A Father's "Good Gifts"
The Story of Jesus' Father and Us

This is it, the final devotional in a month of loving and learning from some of the famous and infamous fathers of the Bible. It's been quite a read. We've ended in the New Testament, where there appears to be a paucity of identifiable fathers. At the least, there doesn't seem to be the intense identification with ancestry that is woven through the Old Testament.

We don't know this, but it appears that those closest to Jesus Christ never fathered children. We only know that Simon Peter was married (and that's because his mother-in-law became ill). Instead, they were a band of brothers with Jesus as their steadfast center.

Jesus was not going to be a father figure to them. Because He began His ministry at thirty years of age, He must have been of their generation. Secondly, Jesus regularly shifts attention from Himself to His Father, who, in turn, is their Heavenly Father.

As Matthew 5 and Luke 11 illustrate, Jesus assumed more the role of the disciples' teacher or, what we might call today, a guidance counselor. Note the space in the text given to teachings on prayer, especially in Luke when one of the twelve came to Jesus asking to be taught how to pray.

Question: Had Zebedee not taught sons John and James how to pray? Answer: Probably not. (And what about Alphaeus? Had he not instructed his son James how to pray? Tradition says it was James the Lesser who made the request of Jesus.)

Question: How did the disciples come to believe

prayer was so important? Answer: They had seen and heard Jesus pray. Jesus' example inspired prayer. Mark emphasized that Jesus prayed at crucial moments—like at the calling of the twelve (Mark 3:13) and the establishment of their mission (Mark 6:30–32).

The prayer Jesus gives (Matthew 6, Luke 11), often referred to as the Lord's Prayer, is a pattern for believers who have already been forgiven of their sins. The prayer's reference to daily forgiveness underscores the necessity of keeping open communion with Father God. In the Luke discourse on prayer, Jesus spends time emphasizing boldness and persistence in prayer—the asking, the seeking, and the knocking.

Then Jesus takes in the whole gathered crowd and specifically addresses fathers, knowing full well that the men in his crowd were receptive to the concept of fatherhood. We can assume that these fathers, whenever they were able, loved to give gifts to their sons and daughters. Like them, Jesus said, their Heavenly Father liked to give good gifts to those who ask him.

As a father and a husband, teach your youngsters about prayer. Let your wife see you lead the family in prayer. Let your family hear their names mentioned in your prayer.

A Father's "Good Gifts"

Think It Over

The Lord's Prayer has become so familiar, we can say it (and probably not pray it) with our brains turned off. For a change, pray it using first person singular pronouns. In a quiet place, with pen and paper, write out this prayer.

Make prayer a part of your daily family life. Read short passages of scripture and pray for real issues pertaining to your family.

It is traditional for Dad to lead this prayer time. Prepare by making a list of family needs; allow time for requests; and encourage your kids to express themselves. You might think about providing a prayer request box so that family members could anonymously share what's on their hearts.

Last but far from least, be sure to prepare your spirit for leading family worship. Pray that God will give you the words to say. . .and patience to allow everyone else to contribute, too.

The LORD hath heard my supplication;
the LORD will receive my prayer.
PSALM 6:9